The City of Big Shoul
Murder, and Mayhem

AMAZING

CHICAGO

Cover photo courtesy from left to right: Louis Armstrong, Getty Images; Francis O'Neill, public domain; Route 66 sign, author; Jane Addams, public domain; Gemini Man, author.

Photos courtesy of the author or in the public domain unless otherwise noted.

Library of Congress Control Number: 2023938696

ISBN: 9781681064758

Printed in the United States of America
23 24 25 26 27   5 4 3 2 1

The City of Big Shoulders,
Murder, and Mayhem

AMAZING

CHICAGO

FEATURING

CHICAGO'S FIRST CON MAN, DEEP DISH PIZZA,
AND "THE CRIME OF THE CENTURY"

DAVID ANTHONY WITTER

REEDY PRESS

Contents

Acknowledgments

This book would not have been possible without the help of the Northwest Chicago Historical Society, the Society of Midland Authors, John Holden, Ryan Graveface, New City, John Hannafin, Sharon Woodhouse, the Jane Addams Hull House, the wonderful photographs provided by Jennifer Ann Stix, and Josh Stevens.

I would also like to thank the individuals and establishments who provided the following images:

- Wolf Point—Courtesy of Windy City Historical Artifacts
- C.D. Peacock—Courtesy of C.D. Peacock
- Jane Addams—Courtesy of Jane Addams Hull House
- Chief O'Neil—Courtesy Chief O'Neil's Restaurant
- Gemini Giant—Courtesy Launching Pad Restauran
- Lyon and Healy Harp—Courtesy National Music Museum
- Al's Beef—Courtesy Al's Beef Chicago
- Malört Bottle and Label—Courtesy C&H Distillery
- Rosa's Lounge—Courtesy Rosa's Lounge
- Photos by Jennifer Ann Stix: Frank Lloyd Wright Home and Detail; Ernest Hemingway Home; Nelson Algren Apartment; Henry Gerber Home; Reebie Moving and Storage Façade and Detail; Hudson Avenue House; Chicago World's Fair Ticket Booth; John Raap Home and Dark Tales Chapter Heading Haunted House.

Introduction

In 1820, when Philadelphia, Boston, and New York City were thriving cities, Chicago was swampland and prairie, inhabited mostly by Potawatomi Indians.

The City of Chicago was incorporated in 1837, but it was still a swampy backwater. Germans and Irish immigrants began to settle there and the city grew, in part with the opening of the Illinois and Michigan or I&M Canal that connected the Great Lakes to the Mississippi River. Then came the railroads. Located in the center of the country on waterways, Chicago became a railroad hub of the nation. In 1833, Chicago had 333 inhabitants. By 1871, it was 334,774. In 1910, it had reached 2.2 million. Chicago's population grew in part because of the massive numbers of immigrants who arrived in the city from all parts of Europe, as well as the Great Migration of African Americans from the South. These cultures provided a great tapestry in the areas of food, architecture, and the arts. Chicago also spawned many unique individuals who shaped Chicago's history. But with this great wave there also arose a continuing culture of corruption, crime, and vice. This book will detail the lives of the infamous gangsters and murderers who stained Chicago's past with blood, as well as the evil and hauntings whose specter still occupies parts of the city. Nevertheless, the city maintains vibrant links to its past. Some are somber, such as historic cemeteries, while others are reminders of the joy and fun that have made Chicago such a wonderful city. This book will explore not only the well-known symbols of the Windy City, but also the unknown, secret, and odd that make this city . . . Amazing Chicago.

The iconic Chicago Theater sign is a symbol of the city's historic past.

Chapter 1

Chicago: City Firsts, People, Places, and Things

We now see Chicago as a great metropolis, a skyline filled with high-rises and architectural wonders that rival those of any city in the world. But it wasn't always this way. Once, Native Americans roamed the prairie, their teepees placed on the sites of what are now the Wrigley Building and the Willis Tower. Trappers came to trade, drink whiskey, and eat salmon. Chicago's first three businesses, The Wolf, Green Tree, and Sauganash Taverns, catered to them. But soon men brought families, and with this came a need for churches, more civilized amenities, and even fine jewelry and china, the latter being provided by C. D. Peacock Jewelers, which opened in 1837. Soon the muddy ruts were replaced with wooden-plank roads, which in turn gave way to wooden block roads, brick roads and alleys, and now the massive entanglement of concrete. The Chicago River underwent a similar transformation, seeing first the trappers' canoes and skiffs, followed later by schooners, fishing boats with sails, steamboats, massive barges carrying material to the giant smoky factories that lined the river, and eventually the pleasure and tour boats of today. Everything has to start somewhere. Some person, place, or thing has to take that risk. Here is the story of the Chicagoans who did.

Chicago's First Settler

Looking out at the area near Michigan Ave., Wacker Dr., and the Chicago River you can see throngs of cars, buses, pedestrians, and bicyclists so numerous that sometimes movement becomes impossible. On warmer days the river is filled with tour boats, water taxis, pleasure boats, and even kayaks. This is all bordered by magnificent stone buildings and glass towers that surround the intersections like mountains over a valley.

When Jean Baptiste Point du Sable arrived here in 1789, there was nothing save trees, high grass, and water as far as the eye could see. The area was bustling with life, but it was in the form of hundreds of species of birds along with beaver and muskrat on the shore where the river meets Lake Michigan, and deer, bear, and wolves roaming the land. Of African descent and born to a Haitian slave, du Sable traveled up the Mississippi River from New Orleans via Peoria, where

The Jean Baptiste Point du Sable Monument honors Chicago's first settler

he met and married a Native American woman. Able to speak English, Spanish, French, and several Native American dialects, du Sable traded with French, British, and Native Americans. Soon his humble shack turned into a small estate, with a five-room cabin, smokehouse, pens for livestock, two barns, a horse drawn mill, stables, and several smaller houses for his growing family, visitors, and employees.

According to a bill of sale discovered in Detroit in 1913, du Sable sold his property and possessions to Jean La Lime, who later became the first man to be murdered in Chicago. It is not known why du Sable left his magnificent estate. Some say he was disappointed at not being elected Indian Chief, while others say it was just wanderlust. But as he and his family loaded up their wagons or canoes to head southward, du Sable certainly had no idea of what was to become of the area over the next two centuries. His life is now commemorated by a plaza and bust at his former homestead at Michigan and Wacker, and several major city structures, including what was formerly Lake Shore Drive, are named in his honor.

A Statue with a View

Located at Michigan Ave., Wacker Dr., and the Main Branch of the Chicago River, the area around the du Sable monument may boast the best view in all Chicagoland. To the east along the Chicago River are shiny new hotels that lead to Lake Michigan. To the north along Michigan Ave. is Chicago's "Magnificent Mile." To the south is Chicago's famous Loop, and to the west is a line of 20th-century bridges draped across the river, surrounded by buildings of both stone and gleaming glass, lined up one after another as far as the eye can see.

The First Europeans Landed Here

In 1673, explorers James Marquette and Louis Joliet were looking for a way to connect the Great Lakes to the Mississippi River. Here the Des Plaines River turns away from Lake Michigan toward the Mississippi River. After a long portage the explorers discovered this route, which was one of the early keys to Chicago becoming the major transportation hub of the Midwest. Today, the spot is commemorated by a steel sculpture featuring Father Marquette, Joliet, and a Native American guide pushing a canoe through the high grass and swampy wetlands. Hidden near Harlem and Archer Ave., the steel sculpture, now rusted to a fine brown patina, is off the beaten path and unknown by most except for the local birdwatchers who visit the area. A National Historic Site, it is surrounded by 300 acres of forest preserves and wetlands. Now just a sliver of land surrounded by busy roads, railroad tracks, and industrial buildings, the area gives a tiny glimpse of what it must have been like almost 400 years ago.

There is another monument to the explorers. Located at 2816 S. Damen Ave., it features a relief of Marquette speaking to a Native American along the river route. The Art Deco–style cement pillars have a bronze plaque underneath that reads: "James Marquette, French priest of the Society of Jesus, on his mission to the Illinois Indians, spent here the winter of 1674–1675. His journal first brought to the world's attention the advantages of soil, climate and transportation facilities in the Mississippi Valley and the Great Lakes basin." It was created by artist E. P. Seidel and commissioned in 1930 by Mayor William Hale "Big Bill" Thompson. It stands alone in what is now an industrial area that was once a marshland near the Chicago River but is now filled in by road. Just like the other monument on Harlem Ave., its location is on a very busy street near the I&M Canal. For every 100 cars and pedestrians that pass it, perhaps one person will notice the monument.

A third monument is a bronze statue near 24th and Marshall Blvds. According to WBEZ radio, The Marquette Monument was designed by Hermon Atkins MacNeill and dedicated in 1926. Over 15,000 school children had signed a petition asking for such a statue. Marquette and Joliet are also memorialized in many more ways, including Marquette Park in Chicago and the city of Joliet, which is named after the explorer. There are also many more tributes to the explorer throughout the Midwest, including Marquette University in Milwaukee, Wisconsin.

Du Sable certainly had no idea of what was to become of the area over the next two centuries. His life is now commemorated by a plaza and bust at his former homestead at Michigan and Wacker, and several major city structures, including what was formerly Lake Shore Drive, are named in his honor.

Monument to explorers
Father Jacques Marquette
and Louis Joliet

Chicago's First Business

It is 1828. "Chicago" is nothing but a vast wetland. Besides the Potawatomi and a few settlers, the only people in the area are trappers and fishermen, traveling mostly by canoe. While paddling, they would often meet at the junction of the north, south, and main branches of the Chicago River, or the Y. Over time James Kinzie, the son of John Kinzie, Chicago's first white settler, began to notice these gatherings and realized that these men may need a place to rest. So, in 1828, he opened the Wolf or Wolf Point Tavern at this junction. It was an immediate success, as one can only imagine on winter nights how men in primitive fur coats with shoes made of animal fur welcomed a warm fire and meal after being in the wilderness. Kinzie enlisted Billy Caldwell and Samuel Miller to manage the business, and on May 2, 1829, the Peoria County Court issued Chicago's first tavern license for a tavern called Wolf Point. There are many stories behind the name. The area was then filled with wolves that often howled into the night. In her book *Wau-Bun*, Juliette Kinzie says it was named after a local Native American named Mo-aw-ay, or wolf. Nevertheless, a painted sign accompanied by a wolf was hung on the door, and it became Wolf Tavern. Here, settlers ate, drank whiskey, danced, and smoked tobacco. Often, Native American and white men and women danced and drank together, something that was very taboo at the time. The bar was such a success that two years later Mark Beaubien opened his own tavern, The Eagle Exchange. Beaubien was a fiddler who played in front of the fire while his guests drank and danced. A short time later Beaubien expanded the business into a hotel and named it the Sauganash Hotel. A third tavern, the Green Tree

Tavern, was opened by Kinzie in 1833. While the other taverns were demolished, the Green Tree survived until 1933, when the structure made of logs, mud, and wood was taken down. Workers described seeing names, initials, and Native American markings when they disassembled the bar, which had been moved across the river to Fulton and Canal Sts. in 1880.

Today a massive steel and glass high-rise development has been built in the area where the three branches of the river meet. The development is called Wolf Point East and West. It is a far cry from the days when the land was filled with tall grass, water, beavers, and birds.

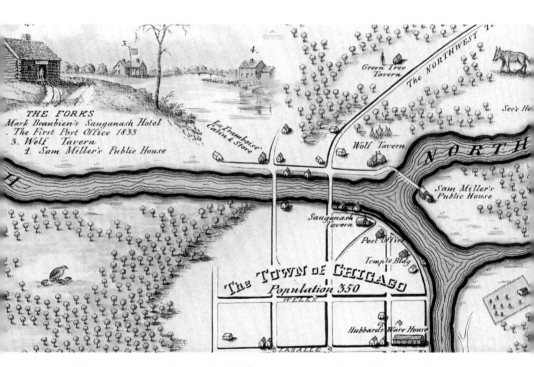

Chicago, circa 1833 showing The Wolf Tavern, Sauganash Hotel/Tavern and Green Tree Tavern, courtesy *Chicago Historical Journal*.

Chicago's First Church

In 1831, Chicago's first church, The First United Methodist Church, was established. Roy Larson, co-author of the book *Born in a Log Cabin*, wrote:

"Our church began in a log cabin, the home of a blacksmith, William See and his wife Minerva. With Beggs preaching and Walker exhorting, eight people joined the church."

In 1838, Rev. Peter Boren inspired 300 people, or one-tenth of the city's current population, to join the church. Boren's words also spurred church members to seek a location away from the unsavory places nearby. That year parishioners rolled the log cabin church to the river, barged it across, and then set it down at Washington and Clark Sts. Now, over 175 years later, the Methodist congregation is still meeting on almost that very spot.

In 1845, the First United Methodist Church moved out of the log cabin and into a brick-and-mortar church. With a spire,

Great Art Lives Nearby

In the plaza just east of the church is *Miró's Chicago* (1981) sculpture; across Washington St. in Daley Plaza is the more famous untitled Chicago Picasso (1967). The landmark City Hall-County building is across the street. The offices of Cook County have the east half of the structure with an entrance on Clark St. The City of Chicago has the west side, and a LaSalle St. address. Next to that, on the northwest corner of Clark and Randolph Sts., is Helmut Jahn's State of Illinois building, now known as the Thompson Center. Public art is one of the great aspects of the city.

The First United
Methodist Church

sanctuary, clock tower, and belfry, the new church was very different from the log cabin.

In 1871, the Great Chicago Fire burned most of the young city, including the first church, to the ground. While the ashes of the fire were still smoldering, Briggs, then 88 years old, stated: "I have seen Chicago come up from the beginning and burn down and rebuilt in every aspect greater than before. It is an utter impossibility to burn pluck, courage, and faith—they are the indestructible gifts of God."

In 1924, the congregation's fifth church building was dedicated. With its magnificent spire, it was the tallest edifice in Chicago at the time. It stands in the center of a teeming metropolis.

The church also contains its own artistic masterworks, including stained glass work detailing the life of Jesus according to the apostles. Other works depict the white and Native American traders, the first log cabin church, Rev. Jesse Walker, the Chicago Fire, and the five First United Methodist Church and Chicago Temple structures that have been a part of the city of Chicago since its first days.

The Noble Seymour-Crippen House

Today you see shows like *Survivor, Alaskan Bush People,* and *Lost,* where people make lives and homesteads while braving the dangers of the wilderness. What you do not see is the camera and crew a few feet away, complete with walkie-talkies and cell phones ready at the first sign of danger. It was not this way for Mark Noble, who arrived in Chicago from Yorkshire, United Kingdom, in 1831 and built a house in the true wilderness in what is now the far northwest side of Chicago. Like most early settlers, Noble first lived around the Wolf Point settlement, renting a cabin from John Kinzie. Noble was a farmer and saw that the swampy land was not suitable for his style of farming and began looking for another location on what he considered to be more solid and fertile ground. He traveled about 20 miles to what is now the far northwest corner of the City of Chicago in what is now 5624 N. Newark Rd. in the Norwood Park neighborhood. Noble claimed 150 acres on Union Ridge. Using wood hewn from the nearby forest and finished in his own sawmill, Noble built what was then a small wooden house approximately 25x30 feet in length. Noble and his wife Margaret lived on the site until Noble passed away in 1839. In 1849, Margaret Noble and Mark Jr. sold the home to Thomas Seymour. As a founding member of the Chicago Board of Trade, Seymour's greater income allowed him to expand the homestead. Additions included a northern wing, servant's quarters, a wraparound porch, and a second floor over the new wing. All were built in Italianate style.

In 1916, the house was purchased by Stuart Crippen and his wife, Charlotte Allen Crippen, a concert pianist and actress.

The family had no steady income, making their living by giving piano lessons in the parlor. Thus, there were few improvements to the house, and it gradually fell into disrepair. The Crippen family owned the property until 1987, when it was purchased by the Norwood Park Historical Society. Through extensive fundraising and the efforts of neighborhood residents, the home was completely refurbished. While keeping the home historically accurate, more modern heating, electrical, and plumbing were added. The house was painted, and the grounds were renovated to include a sloping lawn and renovated clock house. In one nod to the modern era, cement parking pads were poured in the back of the building for visitors and guests. The society regularly conducts tours, historical presentations, and neighborhood events at the house. The Noble Seymour-Crippen House has been named a City of Chicago Landmark and is listed on the National Register of Historic Places.

Chicago's First House, the Noble Seymour-Crippen House

The Second "First House"

At a time when most Chicago homes were log cabins, writer James MacConkey described Greek Revival homes as "a dream of order, balance, and proportion set down in the rude wilderness." This was the home of Henry and Caroline Clarke, who built a home in what was then a swamp near what is now Michigan Ave. and 16th St. The house sat on 20 acres of land in an area so wild that Clarke used it to hunt for game. This was especially necessary after the Panic of 1839, which devastated Clarke's finances. Clarke passed away in 1849, and after that, his wife took over the home. Known as "the widow Clarke," she was mainly responsible for the home's upkeep and many upgrades. New additions included a back portico with Dorian columns, a new porch, and an Italianate cupola. She financed these additions by gradually selling the surrounding land, taking in boarders, as well as taking jobs sewing, embroidering,

and cooking. In 1871, John Chrimes bought the house and moved it south to 46th St. and Wabash Ave. in what is now the Bronzeville neighborhood. This was fortunate as a short time later, the Great Chicago Fire raged through the city, and it would have probably destroyed the home if it had been in its previous location.

In 1941, the home was purchased by the St. Paul Church of God. The church was headed by Bishop Louis Henry Ford, Chicago's first black bishop. Ford took a special liking to the home, caring for it and using his influence to keep it from being torn down. During the 1950s, his wife opened "Chicago's Oldest House Dining Room," which served lunch on weekdays.

The home was moved to the Prairie Avenue Historical District and restored by the City of Chicago in 1980. Today, the Department of Cultural Affairs and the National Society of Colonial Dames use the Clarke House as a museum.

Chicago's First Millionaires Row

The Prairie Avenue Historical District is one of the most significant historical sites in Chicago. During the late 1800s, industrial giants like Marshall Field, Daniel Burnham, and Potter Palmer built massive mansions along Chicago's original Gold Coast. The John J. Glessner house may be the most unique residence still standing. Built like a stone fortress on the outside for fear of anarchists' bombs, it boasts a beautiful inside courtyard where his children could play without fear of kidnapping. The Glessner House is open for regular public tours. Other homes from the golden era of Prairie Avenue include the Keith House at 1901 S. Prairie Ave., the Kimball Mansion at 1801 S. Prairie Ave., and the home of Marshall Field and Marshall Field, Jr., built in 1887. With their mansard roofs, turrets, and towering chimneys, there are few homes like them left in Chicago, or for that matter the entire United States.

Chicago's First Jewelry Store

In 1837, Chicago was still known as the "wild west." The settled parts of the city around Wolf Point were still mostly shacks with wooden plank roads built over swamps. A few brave settlers from cities like New York and Philadelphia, however, began to arrive in the city. While most were single men, many brought their wives. Following their husbands from relatively clean and civilized towns to make a new life, they wanted something to remind them of their old, civilized homes. Elijah Peacock, a watch repairman and jeweler, saw an opportunity to add a touch of class to these primitive surroundings. In 1837, he opened a jewelry store. As the years went on, Chicago's population grew, as did Peacock's business. The railroads began to bring in not only settlers but visitors from smaller rural towns, hoping to bring jewelry, china, and other "civilized" items to take home. Early customers at Peacock's new store included Chicago's wealthiest and most prominent citizens, including Marshall Field, Cyrus McCormick, Potter Palmer, George Pullman, and Mary Todd Lincoln. In 1871, the Chicago Fire burned the city into cinders. Yet Peacock had locked all of his valuable merchandise in a fireproof vault, and in 1873, the business reopened. As time passed, the business passed down to his son, C. D. Peacock. Some of the innovations fostered by C. D. Peacock included being one of the first jewelers to offer a catalog. Customers like Charles Dickens exemplified how the store was becoming world-famous for products by Tiffany, platinum tea sets, and the Peacock Diamond, which weighed 21.81 carats. As time wore on, it was reported that Mick Jagger bought items at the store, arriving not in rock and roll outfits but top hat and tails.

Many Chicagoans and nearby residents of more modest means also shopped at Peacock, as generations of families purchased wedding rings there. Year after year, families would walk by the store or talk of it with gushing memories of the business being part of the most important day of their lives.

In 1993, C. D. Peacock was bought by Seymour Holtzman. The large, grand downtown Chicago store was closed, and the business survived as a stripped down version of its former self, mainly located in smaller stores and kiosks in suburban malls. In 2023, Holtzman transferred the business to his son Steven. Upon accepting his new position, the younger Holtzman and his wife Qi announced that Peacock would soon be opening a large, grand flagship store in suburban Chicago. Displaying renderings of a two-story structure made from stainless steel and glass, the husband and wife team have stated that the store will be part of an effort to link C. D. Peacock to its storied past.

The City Was First Plotted Here

There are over 20,800 blocks, or plotted squares of measured land in Chicago. But on the original map of Chicago, created in 1830, the Varnish Building is located on Block #1. Chicago's first marriage, between Dr. Alexander Wolcott and Ms. Ellen Marion Kinzie, took place on that strip of land on July 20, 1823. Wolcott, after whom Wolcott Ave. is named, was Chicago's first resident physician. A short time later William Ogden, Chicago's first mayor, owned the property. In 1836, Abraham Lincoln's friend and law partner, Grant Goodrich, bought the property. Goodrich later went on to help establish Northwestern University and was one of the leading proponents of the Temperance Movement.

Today, it is best known as the home of Harry Caray's Italian Steakhouse. It was conceived by the Hall of Fame announcer whose career calling games for the St. Louis Cardinals, Chicago White Sox, and Chicago Cubs lasted over 50 years. The Chicago Varnish Company Building, listed on the National Register of Historic Places in 2001, has an even more historic and sinister role as the home and home base for gangster Frank Nitti, which you will read about later in this book.

The Chicago Varnish Building is rich in history.

The First Vertical Lift Bridge

At the beginning of the 20th century, Chicago's industrial power was such that the conflict between railroad traffic and merchant steamships and schooners regularly arose over space not only in the river but also above it. The solution: the first vertical lift bridge. Thus, instead of the two halves of the bridge slowly unfolding like wings, weights and counterweights raised and lowered the entire bridge like an elevator. The giant black iron and cement bridge, now called the Amtrack Bridge, was built in 1915. One hundred and ninety-five feet high with a main span length of 273 feet and a lifting clearance of 130 feet, it is basically two black towers with a moving bar in the middle. As the counterweights are lowered, the bridge rises up above the river so that boats can pass through. There is a little iron "house" perched on top that was formerly the tender station, where an operator would manually raise and lower the bridge. Today it is surrounded by warehouses, apartment buildings, and Chinatown's Ping Tom Park. But this pioneering invention is still ushering in Amtrack Trains more than 100 years after it was built, a reminder of Chicago's industrial past.

Chicago's First Park

Tucked away in a quiet corner of downtown, bordered by 19th-century mansions, bisecting diagonal walks, and picket fencing, and a beautiful reflecting pool surrounding a fountain, you would expect to see Forrest Gump opening a box of chocolates on one of this park's cast-iron benches. Formerly a cow pasture, this three-acre park originated in 1842 when the land was donated by the American Land Company.

Added were trees, intersecting diagonal walkways, shrubbery, and flowers interspaced throughout the park. But the grandest feature was the fountain. Some have described it as a Victorian fountain, but to many it brings forth comparisons to the fountains in the brick courtyard of New Orleans or the famous town squares of Savannah, Georgia. As the 20th century arrived, these elements started to deteriorate from a combination of the

Washington Square Park, also known as "Bughouse Square," is Chicago's oldest park.

weather and lack of upkeep. Yet local citizens and politicians were able to raise $10,000 to restore the park.

It was during this era, after the Haymarket Riots and continuing through the rise of the American Socialist Movement of the 1930s, that the park became a meeting place for leftist orators, artists, poets, Bohemians, and radicals. They would often stand on soapboxes, taking turns speaking before the crowd at a time when Facebook and Twitter were far off in the future. The park gained the nickname "Bughouse Square." There were also oratory contests, and after much debate, the greatest orator was given the title of "king of the soapbox." The park later became a gathering spot for citizens protesting the Vietnam War.

The Last Surviving Member of the Boston Tea Party

It is 1852. Barely 15 years after its incorporation in 1837. Chicago is still a young city. Unlike Boston, Philadelphia, and New York, with their great Revolutionary War battlegrounds and heroes, Chicago has only the site of the Fort Dearborn Massacre, a battle lost to the Potawatomi Indian forces. But on February 25, 1852, Chicago buried its own hero.

David Kennison was the last surviving member of the Boston Tea Party. A great patriot, he also fought at the Battle of Bunker Hill, was a personal scout and spy for George Washington, and accompanied Washington at the surrender of General Cornwallis at Georgetown. Later on, Kennison fought in the War of 1812, where he was wounded. From this he received a pension, which he survived on until the ripe old age of 115.

His burial place is marked by a large stone, bronze plaque, and accompanying sign, placed there by the Daughters of the American Revolution Chicago Chapter. Located in Lincoln Park across the street from the Lincoln Park Farm in the Zoo, it was dedicated with a parade and military honors, and remained even when the cemetery was dug up and moved north as the city limits expanded in 1870. Today, it is often the site of protests by modern day "tea parties" demonstrating against tax increases. It is a monument to rebellion, standing alone in a field of grass and trees in what is now one of Chicago's most upscale neighborhoods.

If the story ended here, it would be a wonderful tale, but that is not the full story. You see, Kennison was at best a fibber and at worst a con artist and liar. Living to 115 is a miraculous feat even with today's modern medicine. Research indicates he was more likely to be 85 (still quite old for the time) when he died. That means he would have been six years old at the Tea Party in 1773 and eight or nine during the Battle of Bunker Hill. Records indicate that he did fight during the War of 1812 and was wounded, but there is no record of him having been at Fort Dearborn, where almost all the soldiers were killed. Arriving in Chicago in 1845, Kennison nevertheless walked around with a vial of tea that he said was saved from the Boston Tea Party and an affidavit saying he was there. In his last years he made his living collecting donations after telling his tales, obviously a better storyteller than hero, but still immortalized with a historical marker placed in Lincoln Park.

Chicago's First Gangster

His gangland reign in Chicago lasted from about 1910 to 1920, but his lifestyle and identity set the mold for gangland figures into the 21st century. It can be said that not only Al Capone, who eventually succeeded him as head boss, but gangsters from Bugsy Siegel to John Gotti followed in his flashy footsteps.

Born in Colosimi in Cozenza, Italy, James "Big Jim" Colosimo immigrated to Chicago at the age of 17 with his parents. A petty criminal, he soon fell into the good graces of political bosses Michael "Hinky Dink" Kenna and "Bathhouse John" Coughlin. He was promoted to precinct captain, and the ward bosses looked the other way as he oversaw a ring of petty criminals and thieves. Colosimo's rising income led him to begin dressing in white suits with fancy walking sticks and jewelry. An imposing man, he soon gained work in Chicago's notorious Levee district financing and providing protection for the many prostitutes who worked there. Eventually he married Victoria Moresco, who worked as a madam, and the two expanded their prostitution business earning an estimated $700,000 a month in today's dollars. In an age before television and mass media, Colosimo's criminal empire went largely unnoticed. But his power over Chicago's illegal gambling in the form of street lotteries, card and dice games in the back rooms of bars, and the lavish poker games where many of Chicago's best-known businessmen gathered was vast. So too was the prostitution and vice in the Levee district, which occupied several city blocks. He opened a nightclub bearing his name at 2128 S. Wabash Ave. that soon became the go-to place for opera stars, politicians, and celebrities. Setting the tone for generations of gangsters to follow, Colosimo rode around town in a chauffeur-driven Pierce-

James "Big Jim" Colosimo was Chicago's first big-time gangster and predecessor to Al Capone.

Arrow and played opera music on the recently invented Victrola while he smoked cigars in his luxurious villa. He also divorced his wife and took up with a young starlet, marrying opera singer Dale Winter, who was decades his junior. Colosimo warded off extortion threats by the Sicilian "Black Hand" through the efforts of New York gangster Johnny Torrio, who brought a young man named Al Capone from New York to work in Colosimo's bars. In 1919, Prohibition was on the horizon. Torrio saw this as a new stream of income, but Colosimo would not open up the gang's purse strings to finance liquor operations. Loyalty never stood in the way of "business," and Colosimo was gunned down in his own restaurant in 1920. Everyone suspected Torrio and his new bodyguard Capone, but no charges were brought. Colosimo's nightclub, however, lasted at the same location until the late 1940s.

Deep-Dish Pizza Is Born

The image of a steel spatula under a slice of deep-dish pizza, melted cheese stretching as it's served, has come to symbolize the windy city as much as The Old Water Tower or Lake Michigan.

The story of the dish that has become a part of Chicago's identity began at Pizzeria Uno at 29 E. Ohio St. Being the first, it is also Chicago's oldest pizza parlor. From its humble beginnings, "Uno's" now has over 200 franchises in 30 states, Puerto Rico, South Korea, and the United Arab Emirates. The restaurant was opened by Ike Sewell and Ric Riccardo. Sewell was a returning Army veteran who had been exposed to the dish in Italy, where it was served as an appetizer.

But Sewell figured that if you simply increased the size and portion of the cheese, sausage, and crust, it would become a meal.

At first, there were problems with the invention. In order for the thicker crust and other ingredients to be cooked fully, they must be heated longer and more evenly. So instead of placing the pizza directly in the oven, it was cooked in a thick, cast-iron pan. This also kept the dough and other ingredients from shifting. Also, the thick layer of cooler, moister tomatoes was placed on top of the pie, insulating the cheese so that it still melted but didn't burn. Others credit Lou Malnati Sr., who was Uno's head cook, with coming up with the first deep-dish pizza recipe.

In today's world of the Food Channel and the billion-dollar cookbook industry, it is quite possible that somebody who is not of a particular ethnic heritage can become a chef of its cuisine. However, in 1943, pizza—and for that matter spaghetti, tomato sauce, Italian sausage, and mozzarella cheese—was very hard to buy of outside of Italian neighborhoods in the United

States. So, it makes sense that somebody of Italian heritage would have had to play some part in the invention of deep-dish pizza. Today, Uno's biggest competitor is the pizza chain started by Lou and his son Rudy, Lou Malnati's. Like Pizzeria Uno, Lou Malnati's pizza is franchised throughout the country. Both claim to be the inventors of deep-dish pizza, but with new franchises continually opening, it seems there is room for both.

Frozen and Thin Crust Too

For those who do not favor deep-dish pizza, Chicago's Home Run Inn is famous for their thin crust pizza. It also has a claim to fame as one of the first pizzerias in the country to offer frozen pizzas.

LGBTQ Pioneer Home

In 1924, Henry Gerber lived in this house at 1710 N. Crilly Ct. It was during this time that he founded the Society for Human Rights (SHR), an organization advocating for the civil rights of homosexuals. It was the first gay rights society in the United States. When the Society for Human Rights began publishing a magazine dedicated towards the gay community, the address on Crilly Court was listed on its charter page, thus giving it a historical imprint. Born in Bavaria, Gerber immigrated to the United States through Ellis Island in 1913. Gerber enlisted in the US Army in 1917 but, perhaps due to his background, refused to fight in the war and was instead sent to an internment

camp in Georgia. In 1925, Gerber established the society, but shortly afterwards the house at 1710 N. Crilly Ct. was raided by the police. He and several other members were arrested, and all material relating to the organization was confiscated. Through the remainder of his life, however, Gerber secretly contributed to many gay publications and magazines. Due to the significance of this organization in the fight for gay rights, the Henry Gerber house was designated a National Historic Landmark in 2015. The National Park Service stated: *Because artifacts of gay and lesbian history are so frequently lost or hidden, the Henry Gerber House stands as an exceptional example of a tangible place of American LGBTQ History.*

Chicago Hot Dog Invented Here

The Chicago-style hot dog is the first and oldest entry in Chicago's iconic street cuisine. While the Vienna beef sausage was introduced at the 1893 Columbian Exhibition, it is said they had introduced the hot dog in New York in the early 1860s. Long and thin, they were said to resemble dachshunds, which might be how they got their name. At first, it was a traditional German sausage served with spicy brown mustard and, in New York, sauerkraut. This was probably how it was originally eaten in Chicago. The addition of the bun came after K. Feuchtwanger, a St. Louis vendor, became tired of people walking away with the gloves he handed out to hold the hot sausages and started serving them on rolls.

The Chicago hot dog added even more to the traditional pickle, lettuce, tomato, and sometimes sport peppers, cucumber, and celery salt, all served on a poppy seed bun. Like many complex recipes, the Chicago hot dog evolved slowly. But if you were to pick one pivotal moment, it was in 1929. That was the year Abe "Fluky" Drexler started to sell Vienna franks out of a hot dog cart in the heart of Chicago's famous Maxwell Street Market. That was the year that sparked the beginning of the Great Depression. Money and work were scarce, especially for folks who did their shopping on Maxwell St. But Drexler had an idea: add vegetables, like onions, relish, pickles, and tomato and turn it into a "meal on a bun."

Throughout the years, the Chicago hot dog and the hot dog stand became a staple on almost every neighborhood street corner. Some of the more famous ones today include Dave's Red Hots at 3422 W. Roosevelt Rd., Jim's Original at 1250 S. Union Ave., Jimmy's Red Hots at 400 W. Grand Ave., Byron's at 1017 W. Irving Park Rd., The Weiner's Circle (famous for the employees insulting the customers) at 2622 N. Clark St., and Gene and Jude's at 2720 N. River Rd. in River Grove, Illinois, just down the road from Chicago. Fluky's is now run by Drexler's son Jack, but instead of being located on the street, the Fluky's brand continues in a Walmart, just outside the city limits at 5630 W. Touhy Ave. in Suburban Niles.

In the past few years, the "Chicago Hot Dog" has gained national acclaim, as it is the subject of numerous books, television travel segments, and "Chicago hot dog" stands are opening across the nation.

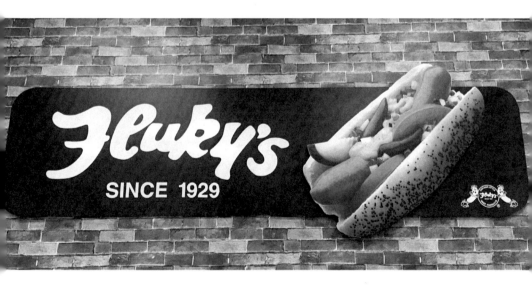

A young Jane Addams, who would go on to establish Hull House.
Photo courtesy of Jane Addams Hull House

Chapter 2

Famous People You May or May Not Know About

Chicago is not New York, a city that spawned or became home to many of our political figures, artists, and historical figures. Nor is it Virginia, birthplace of our greatest leaders, or Los Angeles, home of movie stars, rock stars, and people who now have millions of followers on social media. But throughout its history Chicago has seen greatness. Some, like Frank Lloyd Wright, Ernest Hemingway, or the Obamas, you know about. Yet there are also others—immigrants, women, African Americans, politicians, artists, and just plain characters—that you may not be as familiar with. The stories and identities of people like Francis Willard, Jane Adams, and Muddy Waters are woven into the tapestry of this city. Their lives and causes are noble, often involving the poor, unrepresented, and downtrodden. Some have risen from the ranks of the poor themselves, reaching noble heights through sheer hard work, determination, and sometimes artistic gifts. Others came from wealth but chose to spend their careers helping those less fortunate. But all are part of Chicago and helped to shape its modern identity.

Chicago's First White Settler and Murderer

Today, John Kinzie is honored by having one of Chicago's major streets named after him, and he is still seen as one of Chicago's founding fathers. It is more than ironic, however, that Kinzie was also Chicago's first murderer and sold whiskey, setting the tone for generations of "Chicago's leading citizens" of fame and infamy to follow. Born in Quebec City, Canada, in 1763, Kinzie was already trading and speaking the dialects of the Miami Indian tribe while still in his teens. He slowly journeyed southward, settling in Fort Wayne, Indiana, in 1879. Local laws and increasing settlement made his trading more difficult, and Kinzie continued to journey west, stopping in what was later to become Chicago. He put down roots near Wolf Point, marrying Eleanor Lytle Mc Killip in 1798. In 1804, Kinzie purchased the home of Jean La Lime, making him Chicago's first permanent white settler. Kinzie also began to buy large parcels of land, mostly around the Chicago River. Some early reports stated Kinzie did not offer many sellers a fair price, relying on whiskey and trickery to obtain deeds to land. In 1812, Kinzie and his assistant and landman Jean La Lime were seen quarreling. Early reports written by sources such as Kinzie's daughter in her book *Wau-Bun*, state that La Lime attacked Kinzie with a knife and Kinzie was simply defending himself. Later records indicate that La Lime began to disagree with Kinzie's swindling of Native Americans and others in land deals and selling inferior goods at inflated prices to the soldiers at Fort Dearborn. Most historians also believe the act was Chicago's first murder.

JOHN KINZIE
DECEMBER 23, 1763
JUNE 6, 1828

During the War of 1812, Kinzie was arrested for selling gunpowder and whiskey to both the British forces and the United States Army, making him a traitor to both sides. The British took notice of this and charged him with treason. In 1813, the British captured him and sent him on a journey to England, where he was to be imprisoned. Yet a storm sent the ship crashing against the rocks in Nova Scotia, and Kinzie was able to escape. After the War of 1812 ended, Kinzie continued to buy land and acquire wealth. John Kinzie died in 1828. His body was originally buried in Fort Dearborn Cemetery in what is now Lincoln Park. His remains were later moved to Graceland Cemetery at 4001 N. Clark St. Though he is recognized as one of Chicago's leading citizens and historical figures, it seems only fitting that Chicago's "First White Settler" also sold whiskey and was a murderer.

The "Little Giant"

In 1858, in seven locations throughout Illinois, the diminutive Stephen A. Douglas stood next to the towering figure of Abraham Lincoln in what were to be known forever as "The Lincoln-Douglas Debates." What might not be so well remembered is that Douglas was victorious in the senate race between the two, effectively "winning" the debates and becoming an Illinois Senator. Douglas was known to be, if not pro-slavery, then leaning in that direction. He continually favored compromises between the slave and non-slave states. In the 1860 presidential election, Douglas ran as the Democratic nominee for president against Republican Abraham Lincoln. He may well have won if not for the "Southern Democrats" nominating John C. Breckenridge. Breckenridge and Whig candidate John Bell effectively split the Democratic vote, allowing Lincoln to win.

At the start of the Civil War, Douglas sided with the union and remained a revered figure in Illinois politics. After Douglas death in 1861, a monument was proposed—a giant statue, which today stands over Lake Shore Dr. near 35th St. Construction of the 96-foot-tall granite structure was begun in 1866 and completed in 1881. Three circular bases are topped by a 20-foot-diameter octagonal mausoleum. Inside, a Vermont marble sarcophagus holds Douglas's remains, surmounted by a marble bust of the Senator. At the top is a nine-foot statue of "The Little Giant."

A tall monument to Stephen A. Douglas, Chicago's "Little Giant," on Chicago's South Side

Ernest Hemingway's Birthplace

His prize-winning books took place in revolutionary Spain, the plains of Africa, the streets of Paris, and the wilderness of the American west, but Ernest Hemingway was born and raised in the quiet, suburban town of Oak Park, just outside Chicago's city limits. Today his birthplace is an historic landmark and museum.

Ernest Hemingway was born in 1899 to his mother Grace, a music instructor, and father Clarence, a physician. The large, Queen Anne–style house where Hemingway lived the first six years of his life was owned by his grandparents, Caroline and Ernest Hall and also served as an office for his father's work. The house is large, with a wraparound front porch, large den and dining room, and bedrooms in addition to Dr. Hemingway's office on the second floor. Although there were few restaurants at the time, the kitchen is relatively small. The house was sold in 1905, forcing the Hemingways to move. In later years it served as a rooming house, and much of the home was reconfigured to add rooms and bathrooms. The house  was purchased by the Ernest Hemingway foundation of Oak Park in 1992. The group gradually and meticulously restored the home to the way it was during Hemingway's early years. In 2001, the home became a museum open to the public. Tours are available on Fridays and Sundays from 1:00 p.m. to 5:00 p.m. and on Saturdays from 10:00 a.m. to 5:00 p.m.

America's Greatest Architect

Although the man often called America's greatest architect designed houses throughout America and even Japan, there is no doubt that the greatest concentration of Frank Lloyd Wright homes is in Oak Park, Illinois. And it is no wonder, as the famed architect lived there from 1889 to 1909. When he moved into his home in 1889, Wright was still working for Louis Sullivan, but in order to finance his new family and his own expensive tastes, Wright began to take outside commissions. Sullivan fired Wright, who then used this freedom to create what is now known as the Prairie School of Architecture. Many of his greatest early designs line the streets of Oak Park, easily within walking distance of his home and studio. They include the Harry S. Adams House, the William E. Martin House, the Robert B. Parker House, the Nathan G. Moore Home, and the spectacular Arthur B. Heurtley House, which is located just blocks from Wright's home and studio. All in all, Wright designed or remodeled 25 houses in Oak Park. This includes, of course, his own home and studio. As in many of his designs, the outside of his home features vertical lines that stretch to the horizon and a color scheme that blends with nature. But it is the main living room's barrel-vaulted ceiling, with its roof and sides containing Wright's trademark–stained glass windows, a fireplace, and glistening oak floors that tell you why this man is still known as the greatest architect in the nation.

After 1909, Wright began to get commissions from all over the nation and the world, including the Imperial Hotel in Japan, the San Marcos Desert Resort in Arizona, the Taliesin in Wisconsin, and his most famous work, the Fallingwater House in Pennsylvania. By the 1960s, the Oak Park residence

The Frank Lloyd Wright Home and Studio Museum in Oak Park, Illinois

and workshop had fallen into disrepair. In 1974, the house was taken over by the National Trust for Historic Preservation, which gradually restored it to its original grandeur. Today it hosts the Frank Lloyd Wright home and museum which is a National Landmark open for tours year-round.

America's First Female Nobel Laureate

During an era where poverty was rampant in Chicago, Jane Addams was a champion for women's rights, workers' rights, and the poor, especially children. Her efforts changed the way these groups were treated in Chicago and across America, earning her the distinction of being the first American woman to win the Nobel Peace Prize.

Born into a wealthy family, Addams visited England after college in 1887. There she was exposed to the starving poor on the streets of Charles Dickens's London. At the same time, she visited Toynbee Hall, a settlement house on the cutting edge of what was to become the social reform movement. Returning to Chicago she saw that the newly arrived Italian, Greek, Jewish, and other immigrants were in much of the same situation as those in London. In response, she and classmate Ellen Gates Starr opened Hull House. Hull House offered children and young adults food, shelter, medical services, schooling, athletic activities, a library, and arts classes. In later years, she established a summer camp where children from the crowded and dirty slums saw and interacted with nature for the very first time. If that was not enough, Addams was a major fighter for women's suffrage, the eight-hour workday, and workers' safety. She also co-founded the American Civil Liberties Union

Haunted Hull House

As one of the oldest buildings in Chicago, Jane Addams's Hull House, built in 1856 at 800 S. Halsted St., has also become one about which tales of hauntings abound. The first apparition seen was that of Irene Donner, who was shot in front of the building by her former fiancé. There is also the famous "Lady in White." This apparition, of a lady in a white dress roaming the halls, was even commented on by Addams herself. Although for many years the Jane Addams Hull-House Museum tried to shy away from these stories, they eventually published a section on the supposed hauntings, from which Addams was quoted as saying, "I can see why the people living in the attic always keep a pitcher of water by the back stairs . . . it is said that ghosts cannot cross running water." But the most enduring may be that of the "Devil Baby." The story goes that a pregnant woman's husband tore a holy picture from the wall, saying he didn't care if the devil himself was born into their child. Months later, a baby with a red face, horns, and cloven hoofs was born. The baby was then taken to Hull House, where it is said people lined up for blocks to see the child, who, some say, was the inspiration for the film, *Rosemary's Baby*. While Jane Addams was disgusted by these stories and turned people away, gawkers and ghost tours continue to visit the site to this day.

and was a charter member of the National Association for the Advancement of Colored People. The hard work, kindness, and vision of Jane Addams improved the lives of thousands of Chicagoans for generations.

The Police Chief Who Saved Irish Music

He was Chicago's Superintendent of Police between 1901 and 1905 and was known as one of the few honest policemen in a city of vice. Yet Francis O'Neill will be revered forever by musicians and members of the Irish community worldwide as one of the greatest chroniclers and promoters of traditional Irish music. Francis O'Neill was born near Banty, County Cork, Ireland, and he heard and played Irish music growing up. At 16, he sailed off on an English merchant vessel. Circumnavigating the globe, he was shipwrecked in the Pacific only to be rescued and brought to San Francisco. In his new country, he worked as a cowboy in Montana and a laborer in New Orleans and Missouri before ending up in Chicago as a sailor on a Great Lakes shipping vessel. He ended up in a profession common to many Irish immigrants in Chicago, a policeman.

His devotion was shown when he was shot in the back and still brought in a murder suspect, and O'Neill quickly rose through the ranks to become Superintendent of Police in 1901. He was steadfastly honest during a period where corruption and vice ruled Chicago. He did use his power as chief to bring over many of Ireland's finest musicians, promising them jobs on the police force. A flautist, fiddler, and piper, he also began collecting anything to do with Irish music. In 1903, he published *The Music of Ireland*, which contained sheet music for 1,850 melodies. After retiring, he wrote six more books on Irish music, including *The Dance Music of Ireland, 400 Tunes Arranged for Piano and Violin,* and *Waifs and Strays of Gaelic Melody.* O'Neill's story had been largely forgotten, but he has been rediscovered in the new Millennium. Three books on his life have been written since 2000, the most recent being *The Beat Cop: Chicago's Chief O'Neill and the Creation of Irish Music,* by Michael O'Malley in 2022. In 2012, the play, *Music Mad; How Chief O'Neill Saved the Soul of Ireland,* was performed. In Ireland, he is memorialized by a statue in his hometown, Trailbane, County Cork. There is also a detective named "Chief" O'Neill in the long-running television show, *Chicago PD.*

History in a Pint

Chief O'Neill's is an Irish pub and restaurant at 3471 N. Elston Ave. on Chicago's north side. Besides serving Irish beers like Guinness and Harp, the restaurant features traditional dishes like fish and chips and shepherd's pie. There is also a memorial or small museum dedicated to O'Neill containing photos, books, and personal belongings.

She Changed the "City of Booze"

Many are familiar with the image of Carrie Nation, the axe wielding, bottle smashing temperance warrior of Kansas. Yet Chicago had its own citizen who became a national leader of the Temperance Movement, in a more subdued and perhaps more effective way.

Frances Willard, President of WCTU/ Women's Suffrage Advocate. Courtesy of the author's collection

Frances Willard was the former Dean at the Woman's College at Northwestern University, which was then a strict religious institution. A few miles south in Chicago, newly arrived immigrant men toiled in factories up to 12 hours a day and often lived in slum-like tenements filled with rats and filth. As a result, many turned to alcohol, but the temporary relief often turned into domestic abuse of wives and children. Willard saw firsthand the results of this, stating: "Alcohol is the demon which transforms plenty into poverty, happiness into horror, genius into imbecility, and hope to despair." Joining the Woman's Christian

The former home and office of Frances Willard is now a museum.

Temperance Movement, she served as secretary but quarreled with then-President Annie Wittenmyer. In 1881, she ran against her and won. Willard began to transform the organization. Its membership rose from 22,800 to 138,377 within a few years, and the group had to expand from its headquarters in Willard's home in Evanston. So, Willard raised $1,500,000 to build a magnificent headquarters at Monroe and La Salle Sts. Twelve stories high with 300 offices, it was called The Woman's Temple. Besides the WCTU offices it now houses the National Bank of America, The Bank of Commerce, the Metropolitan National Bank, and the Bank of Montreal. It was the first major urban building in the nation built by women and dedicated primarily to women's rights and causes.

Willard died in 1897. Sadly, she didn't live to see the passing of the 18th Amendment to the US Constitution, which outlawed alcohol, as well as the 19th Amendment granting women's suffrage, two major laws she had a significant part in creating. During her lifetime, Willard was also a major force in educational, labor, and prison reform, and she eventually saw alcoholism not as a crutch for the morally weak but as a disease that ruined a person's health. Willard also campaigned against the many traveling "elixir salesman" of the era, who traveled in covered wagons with plaques containing fake doctoral degrees selling bottled "cures" for alcoholism.

"Satchmo" in Chicago

Louis Armstrong, the "The King of Jazz," was born and raised in New Orleans, the birthplace of jazz, and the city has an airport, park, and other civic entities that bear his name. Yet for many jazz scholars, his years in Chicago, from 1922 to 1929, was the period of his greatest personal and artistic achievement.

Armstrong arrived in Chicago by train on July 8, 1922. He traveled there to play with King Oliver and the King Creole Jazz Band. Growing up an orphan on the streets of New Orleans, Armstrong had the talent but lacked confidence and polish, both musically and personally. While living in Chicago, Armstrong not only broke away from his mentor, King Oliver, but also broke out of the Dixieland style, whose structured format was good for ensemble musicians, but tended to deny exceptional musicians like Armstrong the freedom to shine.

While in Chicago, Armstrong formed the "Hot Five," and the "Hot Seven," still considered among the greatest and most influential jazz bands of all time. It is also in Chicago where his solos on songs like "Struttin' with Some Barbecue," "Cornet Chop Suey," and "Chicago Breakdown" transformed the way soloists played. Before these compositions, jazz followed a set, Dixieland pattern. Armstrong opened up the genre to the improvised solo, which now characterizes the music. During his time in Chicago, Armstrong's deep throated, scatting vocals on songs like "Heebie Jeebies" were also able to take center stage. These compositions made Armstrong a top-selling recording artist and are now recognized as an integral part of American culture of the 20th century.

Louis "Satchmo" Armstrong

Jazz Musician
1898-1971

One of the most gifted musicians in the history of jazz, Louis Armstrong spent his most inventive years— 1925 to 1929—playing the clubs of Chicago's Black Belt, especially the Sunset Cafe. During that time, his bands the Hot Five and Hot Seven recorded 60 performances that transformed jazz, including "Potato Head Blues," "West End Blues" and "Heebie Jeebies."

Louis Armstrong was born in New Orleans into extreme poverty. He learned to play the cornet while serving a sentence for delinquency. After eight years of playing in clubs and on riverboats, Armstrong moved to Chicago to join Joe "King" Oliver's Creole Jazz Band.

Louis Armstrong and the Hot Five: Johnny St. Cyr (banjo), Johnny Dodds (clarinet), Kid Ory (trombone), Lil Harden Armstrong (piano).

In Chicago, Armstrong switched from cornet to the more brilliant-sounding trumpet. He created a sophisticated form of improvisation whose uninhibited tone, range and rhythm revolutionized modern music. He also began his trademark "scat" singing, using his voice as an instrument with nonsense syllables.

In 1925, he married pianist and composer Lil Hardin and they bought this home at 421 East 44th Street. Hardin-Armstrong was a pianist and bandleader as well as a member of Armstrong's Hot Five. Together, Louis and Lil composed many classic jazz tunes.

By the late 1920s, Armstrong began touring internationally. He spent the next few decades as a soloist and singer with various big bands, and appeared in more than 50 films.

Armstrong lived in a rented Greystone at 421 E. 44th St. in the Bronzeville neighborhood, which at the time was the center of African American culture in Chicago. His home was nearly close enough to walk to jazz venues like the Vendome Theater (3145 S. State St.), Dreamland Café (3520 S. State St.), Lincoln Gardens (459 E. 31st St.), and Sunset Café (315 E. 35th St.). It is known that the Sunset was owned by an associate of Al Capone, who was said to have admired Armstrong's style. While living in Chicago Armstrong met and married pianist Lil Harden in 1924. She is said to have furnished the house on 44th St., which featured fine furniture and a private bath, luxuries that Armstrong had not experienced to that point. Armstrong left for New York in 1929 and became the rage of Harlem. Today, Armstrong's rented Greystone home is largely unchanged on the outside and denoted by a historical marker.

The King of Chicago Blues

He is the Mannish Boy, the Hoochie Koochie Man, and the original Rolling Stone. Born on the Stovall Plantation near Clarksdale, Mississippi, Muddy Waters took the field hollers, knife pieces, and acoustic Delta blues of Robert Johnson and Son House, music that was played in train stations and field parties, and brought it north to Chicago. He arrived there in 1943, but by 1944 he had traded in his acoustic guitar for an electric model. In 1948, he had his first hit, "I Can't Be Satisfied," for Chess Records. He later teamed up with songwriter Willie Dixon, who composed a string of songs including "I'm Ready," "Hoochie Koochie Man," and "I Just Wanna Make Love to You."

The Rolling Stones and Muddy Waters

On a clear September day in 1981, a group stood in front of the legendary Checkerboard Lounge in Chicago's Bronzeville neighborhood. They had heard from a friend that somebody had rented $10,000 worth of lighting and sound equipment and sent it to the Checkerboard. The Rolling Stones were touring the United States and the crowd knew that they were the only ones who could toss around that kind of money. They stood in the parking lot from 4:00 p.m. until after dusk hoping to get a glimpse of the World's Greatest Rock and Roll Band. They were there to see The Rolling Stones, but The Stones were there to see Muddy Waters. Word was out that he was ailing, and they wanted to play with him one last time. Unfortunately, the rumors were true; Waters died in 1983. The performance was recorded and portions became part of the DVD, *The Rolling Stones at the Checkerboard Lounge, Live in Chicago 1981.*

This mural of Muddy Waters looms over Chicago's State St.

He continued recording for Chess, with more hits like "Mannish Boy" and "Got My Mojo Workin'". These songs became part of the blues cannon, influencing not only blues musicians, but then-teenagers like Eric Clapton, Mick Jagger, and Keith Richards. Although Waters's records scored high on the Rhythm and Blues charts in the 1950s and early 1960's, Waters did not receive many of the royalties he was due from Chess Records until Waters and Dixon successfully sued Chess in the 1970s. It was also during this time that the blues-rock craze was in full swing. Artists like Johnny Winter used their commercial pull with the major record companies to record and promote Waters's albums like *Hard Again* and *King Bee*. Along with *The Muddy Waters Woodstock Album*, these records were both commercially and critically successful. Between 1972 and 1980, Waters won six Grammy Awards in the Best Traditional Folk category. After his death, Waters was voted into the Rock and Roll Hall of Fame and the Blues Hall of Fame, won a Grammy Lifetime Achievement Award, and was honored with his own US postage stamp.

The Author with the Golden Arm

Nelson Algren once said, "The farther away you get from the literary traffic, the closer you are to sources," and from 1959 to 1975, his main residence was on the third floor of this handsomely decorated three flat. Just three blocks west of Milwaukee Ave., it was then known as "Polish Broadway."

Algren was the chronicler of Chicago's immigrants and the drunks, gamblers, and hustlers who lived in what is now trendy Wicker Park but was then a poor, blue-collar area. His most famous book, *The Man with the Golden Arm*, won the National Book Award in 1950 and was made into a movie starring Frank Sinatra in 1955. It depicted Frankie Machine, a heroin addicted gambler who spent his nights dealing cards and days hanging out in corner bars.

Just a short walk from this apartment lived characters like "Lefty," "Dropkick," "Catfoot," "Little Johnny," "Noseberg O'Brian," "Johnny Polish," "Railroad Shorty," and even Roman Orlov from the Polonia Bar, who was named "the biggest drunk of them all" in the short story, *How the Devil Came Down Division Street*.

Algren also wrote, *Chicago: City on the Make*. A book-length essay that almost reads like an epic poem, it depicts Chicago's history through its people—the immigrants, swindlers, gamblers, and thieves from its first settlers (like John Kinzie), through corrupt politicians and ward healers, early ethnic gangs, the era of Al Capone, continuing into the rough-and-tumble Depression and post-war years when the city grew to a great metropolis, but at the expense of immigrant and black labor. It may be the best prose ever written about Chicago.

Algren talked the talk, but also walked the walk. A habitual gambler, it is said he spent most free afternoons at local racetracks.

Algren's "Bachelor Pad" Landmark

Twice divorced, Algren lived in the apartment on Evergreen with his cat, surrounded by books, manuscripts, and a typewriter from which he produced the greatest stories ever written about Chicago. Today the front of the building is adorned with a plaque and historical marker. There is also a brown, honorary street sign three blocks west at Evergreen and Hoyne, declaring the stretch, "Nelson Algren Avenue."

He also drank more than his fair share. During his lifetime he befriended my very own great uncle, and every Christmas he would stick a bottle of vodka in his mailbox on Forest St. in Miller Beach. It was also in Miller where Algren carried on an affair with famous feminist writer Simone de Beauvoir.

Nelson Algren's former apartment on Evergreen and Hoyne Aves.
Photo by Jennifer Ann Stix

The Obamas' Chicago Roots

Michelle Robinson was born on the south side of Chicago at 7436 S. Euclid Ave. She was the daughter of a city worker who struggled with multiple sclerosis. She attended Whitney Young High School, Chicago's first magnet school, located near downtown Chicago. Robinson commuted three hours each day in order to attend, and distinguished herself by going on to attend Princeton University. While Whitney Young High School had long been known for its racial diversity, it was not the same at Princeton. The parents of her first roommate complained to the university and asked that their daughter, a white girl, not share a room with an African American. Robinson talked of earning a doctorate but was often told instead that she was "setting her sights too high" and should transfer to a smaller, state school, perhaps to become a teacher. Robinson graduated cum laude from Princeton in 1985. She then obtained a law degree from Harvard University, a feat that was not common for African American women. She began working at a large Chicago firm, Sidley Austin. While there, this young, accomplished single woman was introduced to another Harvard graduate and lawyer turned community organizer named Barack Obama. Although Obama was raised in Hawaii, he received his

"On our first date, I treated her to the finest ice cream Baskin-Robbins had to offer, our dinner table doubling as the curb. I kissed her, and it tasted like chocolate."

FROM AN INTERVIEW IN O, THE OPRAH MAGAZINE, FEB. 2007
IMAGE COURTESY OF BLACKPAST.ORG
—PRESIDENT BARACK OBAMA

On this site, President Barack Obama first kissed Michelle Obama

The famous "Kissing Rock" marks the spot where the future president and first lady had their first kiss.

undergraduate degree from the University of Chicago. After attending Harvard Law School, he returned to Chicago, where he became a community organizer and worked with neighborhood and church groups in the Hyde Park neighborhood. He also worked as a lawyer at a major Chicago law firm. Robinson and Obama agreed to meet after work on what was to become their first official date. While strolling through Hyde Park and its surrounding University of Chicago, they decided to stop at a Baskin-Robbins ice cream parlor. Sharing two scoops of ice cream turned into their first kiss.

Today this first kiss is marked by a plaque affixed to a large granite boulder that reads: "On our first date, I treated her to the finest ice cream Baskin-Robbins had to offer, our dinner table doubling as the curb. I kissed her, and it tasted like chocolate."

A Monument of Granite vs. the Birthplace of Love

A few blocks east in Jackson Park, the Barack Obama Presidential Center is being built. A $300 million project—its total cost including improvements to local infrastructure and new housing developments may exceed one billion dollars—it will contain gardens, libraries, public spaces, and a towering building housing Obama's presidential papers, records, and documents. But are these as important as where he fell in love?

The famous "El Train" runs over the Chicago River at the Kinzie Avenue Bridge.

Chapter 3

Iconic Locations and Monuments to Living History

Chicago is nearly 200 years old—very young by the standards of most European cities, and young compared to many in the Northeast and Mid-Atlantic regions of the United States. But compared to cities in the West, and especially the nation's sprawling suburbs, Chicago is an older city filled with precious history. Buildings like the Old Water Tower, Wrigley Field, and the Merchandise Mart are known worldwide. But most in this section, like the Birthplace of Walt Disney, the home where *The Wizard of Oz* was written, or the last wooden house to survive the Great Chicago Fire, may be new to you.

. . . .

When Native Americans Roamed Chicago

Before the white settlers, Chicago's woods, prairie, and wetlands were occupied by Native Americans including the Potawatomi Tribe, which hunted, fished, and camped in the area. Chicago's first permanent white settlers, John Kinzie and his wife, befriended many of these natives. They hunted and fished together, and their children played with one another in the open, often harsh land. During the War of 1812, while the Native Americans attacked and "massacred" the American/white soldiers at Fort Dearborn, Pin Quay spotted his old friend John Kinzie. As an early settler in a barren land, Pin Quay's and Kinzie's children used to play together and both families aided each other during times of disease. Stories differ, but legend has it that Chee Chee Pin Quay assured the attackers that Kinzie was his prisoner and that he would personally scalp the white man. Pin Quay went so far as to put Kinzie in his canoe and raise his axe towards Kinzie's head. But the blow was only glancing, and instead Pin Quay paddled his friend to safety at a US Army fort in Michigan.

Kinzie returned and later became Chicago's richest man and leading citizen. As a reward for saving his life, when Kinzie later became Chicago's largest land owner, richest man, and controlled much of local politics, he used his power to appoint Chee Chee Pin Quay, now also called by the American name of Alexander Robinson, Chief of the Potawatomi Tribe. He also gave him much of the land in what is now the Cook County Forest Preserves, including Alexander Robinson Woods, along the Des Plaines River in areas between Irving Park, Foster,

The Resting Place of Alexander Robinson at 4800 W. River Rd.

Cumberland, and East River Rd.

Robinson and a mixed Native American named Billy Caldwell negotiated the Treaty of Prairie Du Chien in 1829. In return for land cessions, the United States promised the Potawatomi new lands, annuities, and supplies. In what some refer to as a betrayal, Robinson and his family farmed the great amount of land they were given and lived in a house that survived in various forms (the last being a waterbed store) until 2000. Some say he was also given a barrel of whiskey that was to be perpetually refilled. It is also said that upon seeing the devastation of the Great Chicago Fire, the Chief rode his horse downtown gazing at the flattened and smoldering city, and said, "at last, the prairie has been returned."

Today, on the west side of the 4800 block of East River Rd. there is a granite boulder marking the site where formerly stood two headstones of the graves of Indian Chief Robinson and his wife Catherine Chevalier. The boulder is inscribed: "*Alexander Robinson—(Chee-Chee-Pin-Quay)—Chief of the Potawatomi, Chippewa, and Ottawa Indians who died April 22, 1872—Catherine (Chevalier) his wife who died August 7, 1860—And other members of their family are buried on this spot—Part of the reservation granted him by the Treaty of Prairie Du Chien—July 29, 1829, in gratitude for his aid to the family—of John Kinzie and to Capt. and Mrs. Heald at the time of the Fort Dearborn Massacre.*"

The Fort Dearborn Massacre

Dedicated in 1923, this representation of the battle is portrayed in a relief in the concrete tender's house at the Michigan Avenue Bridge. The conflict between United States troops and the Potawatomi Indians took place on August 15, 1812, as part of the War of 1812. When the British captured Fort Mackinac, Fort

Relief depicting the Fort Dearborn Massacre at Michigan Ave. and Wacker Dr.

Dearborn's supply chain was cut off, and the US Army ordered the evacuation of all troops. Surrounded and outnumbered by the Native Americans, commander William Wells negotiated a surrender with Potawatomi Chief Black Partridge. The terms included the US forces safe passage to Fort Wayne in return for leaving their stores of whiskey and gunpowder intact. However, Captain Nathan Heald set fire to the gunpowder and provisions and dumped the whiskey into the river. Chief Partridge tried to control his braves, but angry at the betrayal, they caught up with the US force, which had retreated a short distance to the south. One soldier apparently fired upon the braves, who commenced to attack the party. In the end, Heald detailed the American loss at 26 regulars, including 12 militia, 2 women, and 12 children killed. Twenty-eight soldiers, seven women, and six children were taken prisoner. With the removal of a statue commissioned by George Pulman in 1893 after protests by American Indian groups in the 1970s, this relief is the sole monument to the battle.

The Old Water Tower

It is another Chicago icon, a landmark featured in almost every Chicago promotional video and tourist brochure. But the real story behind the old water tower is as good as its myth. Built in 1869 as a standpipe and pumping station, the structure represented the first step toward ending cholera epidemics by bringing clean water from Lake Michigan into Chicago's homes. Made of Joliet limestone, it resembles a gothic, Medieval fortress, or as Oscar Wilde remarked, "a castellated monstrosity with pepperboxes stuck all over it." The water tower was one of five buildings to survive the great Chicago fire intact. The building was modernized from 1913 to 1916, as every piece of limestone was replaced by volunteers. On October 6, 1971, 100 years after the great fire, the building was designated a Chicago landmark. In the following years, the Old Water Tower and its sister building across the street, the Old Pumping Station, were converted into tourist information centers filled with old photos, videos, and exhibits on Chicago history.

The House That Survived the Great Chicago Fire

The Great Chicago Fire of 1871 turned the city into a mass inferno. Beginning on October 7, flames driven by fierce winds jumped from building to building and from tree to tree, turning the hay and firewood in nearby sheds into fiery dust. For a time, it was thought that the Chicago River would serve as a firebreak, and people dove into the waters to save themselves. But like a fiery trapeze artist, the flames leapt across the river, heading northward. The heat was so intense that it muted the efforts of valiant fire fighters, who had run low on water because of a recent drought.

The fire blazed for three days, devouring everything in its path from Roosevelt Ave. south to Fullerton on the north, and the Lake and the Chicago River to the west. As a merciful rain finally fell on October 10, the city lay in smoldering ruins. Overall, one third of the city was destroyed and 100,000 Chicagoans became homeless. An estimated 300 people lost their lives, and countless livestock also perished. The economic cost was estimated at $200 million in 1871, which would be billions today.

About half a dozen structures survived the fire. The most notable is Chicago's Old Water Tower, which was made of limestone. St. Michael's Church, St. James Episcopal Cathedral, and the Unity Church were left with only their edifice of stone standing. Other churches and even two homes on N. Cleveland St. were scalded by the fire but lay on the edges of its path.

Yet one wooden home was able to survive: the Richard Bellinger house. Located in the heart of what is now Chicago's Old Town

The house at 2121 N. Hudson Ave. survived the Great Chicago Fire.
Photo by Jennifer Ann Stix

neighborhood at 2121 N. Hudson Ave., it was in the direct path of the steamrolling inferno. As orange balls of fire driven by fierce winds devoured the surrounding homes, Bellinger tore up the wooden sidewalks and fences around his property. He then poured buckets of water over the house's walls and roof, and even made a damp moat in the surrounding garden.

Legend has it that when Bellinger ran out of water, he used the hard cider he had in the basement to ward off the flames. With the building already soaked, the Chicago police officer stood watch over his house for three days, using brooms, axes, and blankets to stamp out the small blazes that sprouted like weeds on his rooftop. When the fire was over, his house stood alone amid the burning rubble.

The home, now designated a Chicago landmark, sold for $2,250,000 in 2022. I am sure part of the upkeep includes a modern sprinkler system.

From the Ashes to Hosting Presidents

It is one of the most magnificent hotels in Chicago and also the oldest. In some ways, the story of the Palmer House represents the history of Chicago itself. It was born out of a "blind date" between business magnate Potter Palmer, whose 1858 dry goods store turned into a high-end store that eventually became Marshall Field's, and wealthy socialite Bertha Honore. The date was arranged by Field. Perhaps to impress his future spouse, Potter opened the first Palmer House in September of 1871. Thirteen days later, the Great Chicago Fire burnt it to the ground. Undaunted, Palmer sifted through the rubble, and in one of the most famous displays of confidence of any Chicagoan

The plush lobby of the Palmer House Hotel

in history, he immediately borrowed $1.7 million and declared that he would build a hotel out of the ashes. This deed was one of the key elements in Chicago's survival and amazing resurgence after the fire had left the city in abandoned ruin.

Finished in 1873, the new hotel at State and Monroe Sts. soon became the playground for Chicago's industrial giants, including Field, Joseph Sears, and many others. Adorned in Tiffany chandeliers and gold leaf columns, other notable guests have included Oscar Wilde, Buffalo Bill, Charles Dickens, and

Ulysses S. Grant who had a dinner there hosting 500 guests, including Mark Twain.

The hotel was remodeled again between 1923 and 1929, roaring along with the 1920s and adding "modern" technology, including electric refrigeration, an indoor swimming pool, and updated lighting. Also added was the Empire Room, which hosted legendary entertainers, including Frank Sinatra, Judy Garland, Ella Fitzgerald, Harry Belafonte, Benny Goodman, Louis Armstrong, Sonny and Cher, and Barbara Streisand. By this time, the hotel was now run by Potter Palmer II. During the 1950s and '60s the hotel became a favorite spot for politicians, as it hosted the victory parties for Mayors Richard J. and Richard M. Daley and rallies for Bill Clinton during the 1996 Democratic Convention.

As the nation entered the new Millennium, the hotel once again received a $170 million renovation which was completed in 2009.

The Brownie Was Born Here

For sweet lovers, the Palmer House kitchen is said to be the place where Palmer's wife, Bertha, conceived the idea for the brownie. As the 1893 World's Fair approached, Palmer apparently wanted a chocolate dessert treat that would feature more chocolate than any previous snack for their lavish parties. Almost 150 years later, her creation is still a favorite of chocolate lovers around the world.

Heavenly Harps

Their harps are some of the finest in the world, featured in symphony orchestras and philharmonics and even exhibited in New York's Metropolitan Museum of Art. At the turn of the 20th century, they were the largest music house in the world. It all started when two men, George W. Lyon and Patrick Healy, arrived from Boston on a commission to create a new sales outlet for music publisher Oliver Ditson. Unlike their home city, which had already been in existence for well over a century, Chicago was still a backwater town with muddy streets and primitive services. But it was also a virgin sales territory, where settlers hungered for music and the cultural reminders of the more civilized east. It was hoped that within 10 years they would provide sales of $100,000. Instead, they topped that figure in six months.

This caught the attention of the music world, and after a wise investment in insurance let them rebuild after the Great Chicago Fire, Lyon and Healy were awarded sole possession of territorial sales by Steinway and Sons Pianos. The partners also specialized in the repair of musical instruments. As time went on, they noticed that the harps that were coming into the shop needed continual upkeep and repair. The partners then began building stronger, better sounding harps. Their first harp was crafted in 1889 and was played at Morgan Park High School for nearly 100 years. Yes, 100 years of use in a high school—if that isn't a sign of sturdy craftsmanship, what is? The company continued to sell sheet music, build harps, and supply band instruments to local schools and institutions. They also built guitars under the Washburn name, as well as drums, violins, banjos, organs, pianos, and wind instruments. Yet technology and changing tastes meant a steady decline in sheet music sales as well as the many roles that were formerly taken by trained musicians. By the 1970s, Lyon and Healy began to struggle. Fortunately a competitor, Victor Salvi, the founder of Salvi Harps in Italy, admired Lyon and Healy harps and decided to add Lyon and Healy to his business in 1987. Today, Lyon and Healy continue to supply harps to orchestras around the world.

Courtesy of Lyon and Healy

The Union Stockyards Gate

"Hog Butcher of the World" is not just a line in a poem. At the turn of the 20th century, Chicago's Union Stockyards accommodated as many as 75,000 hogs as well as 21,000 cattle and 22,000 sheep. This accounted for almost 82 percent of the entire butchered meat supply of the United States. All told, as many as 800 million animals were slaughtered at the stockyards by as many as 40,000 workers employed by companies like Armor, Swift, and Wilson. Every day these workers rounded animals up by the thousands and sent them up a ramp. Squealing and crying, they were clubbed or shot to death and then put on the "killing wheel." Here, more workers, knee deep in blood, sometimes half frozen or in factories at over 100 degrees, took hammer, knife, and saw and cut the animals apart in assembly-line fashion, harvesting hoofs, teeth, and innards—"everything but the squeal."

At one time the Union Stockyards and adjacent facilities occupied almost two square miles. While they employed many people and helped Chicago became the turn-of-the-20th-century boomtown, the area was known for its harsh, cruel, and even deadly working conditions. These were highlighted in Upton Sinclair's 1906 book, *The Jungle*. Neighbors in the Bridgeport, Back of the Yards, and Canaryville areas could smell the stench of rotting flesh and meat for miles, especially on hot summer days. As many as 500,000 gallons of bloody wastewater were pumped into the nearby Chicago River every day—so much that the oxygen released by the rotting flesh resulted in the river being known as "Bubbly Creek." As late as the year 2000, the author took a group of science students from nearby Juarez High School to the area. As students removed debris, the river began percolating like a small volcano.

The stockyards' heyday was during and just after World War I. The demand for meat was high, and rail and river were still king. Restaurants, hotels, its own "L" line, and the international amphitheater that hosted everything from livestock shows to The Rolling Stones were built adjacent to the stockyards. For a time, the stockyards were Chicago's most popular tourist attraction. Advances in refrigeration and trucking, as well as the decentralizing of meat plants, led to the slow demise of the stockyards. They were officially closed in 1971. Today they are memorialized by the Union Stockyards Arch, the original gate to the facility where thousands of workers passed through for over 100 years. The limestone arch is crowned by a sculpture of the head of a prize bull, Sherman, named after the Union General, and is a National Landmark.

Lincoln's Tribute Turns to Scandal

Standing Lincoln is an artistic triumph that is also known for the intrigue and scandal that swirled around the public figures involved in its creation.

The statue was designed by the noted sculptor Augustus Saint-Gaudens, who used Lincoln's 1860 life mask as a model. Standing erect with an intent stare, beard and eyebrows bristling, Saint-Gauden's Lincoln has the bearing of a Greek or Roman god.

Lincoln's grandson, also named Abraham Lincoln, unveiled the statue on October 22, 1887. Leonard Swett, a friend from Lincoln's days in Springfield, gave the commemorative address. Lincoln biographer Alexander McClure noted that "of all living men, Leonard Swett was the most trusted by Lincoln." To all appearances, the unveiling was a grand event. Yet lurking below the surface were tragedy, scandal, shady deals, sex, and perhaps even murder.

While alive, Lincoln tried to cover for his friend Swett, whose business affairs were mired in corruption. Rumors of his illegal deals and swindling of associates became an embarrassment to Lincoln. Later, Swett worked as an attorney for the Lincoln estate. In doing so, he betrayed the memory of his old friend, as instead of organizing Lincoln's estate to provide for his widow, Swett helped organize and conduct a hearing that ended up confining Mary Todd Lincoln to an asylum.

The architect for the surrounding pedestal and plaza, Stanford White, engaged in an even greater scandal involving sex, murder, and intrigue that many describe as the most salacious of the era. White designed the first Madison Square Garden, the Vanderbilt Mansion, and the mansion belonging to the Astor family. But he was most remembered for his womanizing. He is said to have invented the "red velvet swing" from which he courted women. Hung from the den of his tower apartment in Madison Square Garden, he claimed the swinging motion served as an aphrodisiac. One of the women White seduced was actress Evelyn Nesbit, whom he met when she was just 16 years old. While watching a play at Madison Square Garden, White was shot by Harry K. Thaw, Nesbit's jealous millionaire husband. The incident and resulting trial were depicted in E. L. Doctorow's novel, *Ragtime*.

Like his uncles, Edward, William, and Theodore, Abraham Lincoln, the grandson bearing the president's name, also died tragically at a young age, 17, not long after the unveiling. Today the statue stands on the grounds of the newly renovated Chicago History Museum, formerly known as the Chicago Historical Society. As the statue calmly and regally overlooks the great expanse of park named after its subject, there is a woeful tale that the granite and marble will never tell.

The statue *Standing Lincoln* looms over the park named in his honor.

The Wreck of the Louisville

Today, thanks to Daniel Burnham, Chicago's lakefront is a series of parks and beaches enjoyed by swimmers, bike riders, walkers, and even furry, four legged friends. But during the 1800s, Chicago's lakefront more resembled Hong Kong Harbor, with schooners, clippers, and others raising sails, and coal-powered steamboats blowing black smoke into the air. The Chicago Riverfront was even more of a montage of vessels, including sailing dinghies, oar boats, rowboats, tugboats, homemade fishing boats, and crude barges fashioned from wooden planks and barrels. Not surprisingly, these vessels had their share of accidents, some of them severe. The most famous of these was *The Lady Elgin*. Often referred to as the "Titanic of the Great Lakes," it went down near the coast of Waukegan at the cost of 300 lives. Other old shipwrecks include the *Louisville*, a 140-foot steamer that weighed over 300 tons and sank on September 9, 1857. Similar to many of the wrecks on the Mississippi River, it was caused by the explosion of high-pressure boilers. The explosion created a mass of ships parts, including pipes, anchor chain, and parts of the hull, which all sank to the bottom of Lake Michigan in a heaping, tangled pile. It is located off the shores of Chicago's southwest side. Other wrecks include the *Wings of the Wind*, a 130-foot schooner that sank in 1866 some three and a half miles off the Wilson Avenue Crib; and the *David Dows*, a five-masted schooner that sank near the *Louisville* in 1889. Today, divers can see many of these wrecks, which, like those in the ocean, are protected by law.

A tower overlooks Lake Michigan, site of many shipwrecks.

The Iconic Chicago Theater

Called "The Unofficial Emblem of Chicago," the sign is probably one of the top five iconic images of the city. But the sign is just the beginning. Built in an era, the 1920s, when movie theaters were grand palaces, the Chicago Theater might be the grandest in the nation. It was built by Balaban and Katz at a cost of $65 million in today's dollars as the showpiece of a national theater chain that once numbered over 100 theaters nationwide. With seating for over 3,500 patrons, it has been called the Versailles of movie theaters. A partial list of performers who have taken the stage include Duke Ellington, Bob Hope, Benny Goodman, John Phillip Sousa, and Frank Sinatra.

The theater began to decline in the 1970s, showing mainly martial arts and action films. But city leaders saw that it was too great of a landmark to be torn down. Beginning in the early 1980s, the Chicago Theater Renovation Group spent over $22 million in today's dollars to completely restore the theater to its past grandeur. Now on the National Register of Historic Places, it reopened in 1986 with a command performance by Frank Sinatra. The theater now anchors a revitalized Loop area with top names performing weekly. Since reopening it has hosted, among others, the Allman Brothers Band, Harry Connick Jr., Aretha Franklin, Alicia Keys, David Letterman, Lyle Lovett, Oasis, Dolly Parton, Prince, Diana Ross, Van Morrison, and Robin Williams.

The Chicago Theater Marquee contains the encircled "Y," which also serves as Chicago's municipal symbol.

Confederate Graves in Chicago?

Marked by a statue of a Confederate soldier and a Confederate flag, Oak Woods Cemetery, at 1065 E. 67th St., contains the largest Confederate burial ground north of the Mason-Dixon Line and the largest mass grave in North America. The site stands next to the graves of many of Chicago's most prominent black citizens in what is a predominantly African American neighborhood. Why? Up to 6,000 Confederate prisoners perished in Camp Douglas, the nation's largest prison camp for captured southern soldiers. The camp was located on land owned by Stephen A. Douglas, not far from the eventual site of the memorial. The monument, which sits at the south end of a lagoon and consists of a statue, four Confederate cannons in front of neatly placed cannon balls, and as many as 4,000 names of perished prisoners etched into the edifice. It is said that at least 2,000 more are buried

The mass Confederate grave at Oak Woods Cemetery

there, but their names could not be determined. The question of their identity may also answer another one—why, especially in this period of monument-defacing and civil unrest, does this Confederate monument continue to stand? The answer may lie in the tragic circumstances of their deaths. The prisoners lived in a crowded hellhole, subjected to not only the brutal Chicago weather but rampant disease and cruel treatment from prison guards who denied them food both out of cruelty and because the guards had little food themselves. In one particularly brutal winter stretch, it is estimated the camp lost 1,000 prisoners. When erected in 1893, the monument was seen as a further sign of healing in a nation still scarred by the Civil War. Today, it stands as a historic reminder of a brutal and tumultuous period in our nation's history.

Chicago History Is Buried Here

Built in 1863, Oak Woods is Chicago's oldest major cemetery. Interred in this graveyard are many of Chicago's most prominent African American leaders, including:

- Harold Washington, congressman and Chicago's first African American mayor.
- Jesse Owens, gold medalist from the 1936 Olympics.
- Ida B. Wells, journalist, political reformer, and suffragette who helped establish the NAACP.
- John H. Johnson, founder of *Ebony* and *Jet* magazines and BET.
- Larry Doby, the American League's first African American baseball player, buried near Bill Veeck, the white owner of the Cleveland Indians who signed him.
- There are also many former gangsters buried here, including Jake "Greasy Thumbs" Guzic, Big Jim Colosimo, Capone's main rival Bugs Moran, and William "Big Bill" Thompson, the mayor who "presided" over Capone's reign.

Musicians including Thomas Dorsey, the "father of gospel music;" Roebuck "Pops" Staples, patriarch of the Staples Singers; Junior Wells, famous bluesman whose stage moves were adopted by Mick Jagger; and Little Brother Montgomery, pianist who served as a link between Louis Armstrong and modern Chicago blues.

The Biograph's Dillinger Alley

On July 22, 1934, tipped off by the infamous "Lady in Red," the FBI gunned down John Dillinger, famous bank robber and Public Enemy #1, in the alley just south of the Biograph Theater. His killing ensured the theater a permanent place in history. It was not legend; it was fact, and I first heard these facts as a child attending grammar school at Louisa May Alcott School about five blocks away from the Biograph. Many of my grade-school friends lived on streets adjacent to the theater. We would play softball, tag football, and most importantly, "Dillinger and G-Man," our own version of cops and robbers, staging the outlaw's death on the very spot in the alley where it occurred. Many tales of Dillinger spread throughout my childhood neighborhood. One old barber said he cut Dillinger's hair. Another old Chinese man sold handkerchiefs said to be soaked with Dillinger's blood. He seemed to have a new supply every year.

Dillinger's legend ensured that Chicago's Biograph Theater would gain national acclaim, but even before then, the theater had a substantial history. It was built in 1914 at 2433 N. Lincoln Ave., a block north of the intersection of Lincoln, Halsted, and Fullerton Aves. At that time, movies were shunned by the established classes, whose members still preferred "legitimate" theater. Most of the customers of early silent film were immigrants who had trouble understanding English dialogue anyway. But while legitimate theaters were often opulent, silent film "Nickelodeons" were usually a large room with a sheet attached to a wall. Not so the Biograph. Architect

Samuel Crowen was hired to design a theater specifically for film. The black, white, and silver marquee combined elements of classical with a style that was to become the rage of the next decade, Art Deco.

In Dillinger's era, it was advertised as "air cooled," and it thrived through the 1950s. As the age of television arrived, many neighborhood theaters were shuddered. The Biograph survived, partially due to its historical significance and partially because it was converted into various forms, including a second-run theater, an art house, and later a legitimate theater, the Victory Gardens. The theater is on the National Register of Historic Places and was designated a Chicago Landmark on March 28, 2001. Along with the legend based on fact, the Biograph's black and white Art Deco façade will always be a part of Chicago's historical landscape.

The Roaring '20s Pool

With terra-cotta fountains, Spanish mosaic tiles, and faux palm trees, the Hotel InterContinental pool is an aqua blue oasis and a time machine straight out of a Rudy Valentino movie. This lavish locale in the heart of downtown Chicago has attracted its share of stars through the years, from the original Tarzan Johnny Weissmuller to swimming pool goddess Esther Williams, Sugar Ray Leonard, Donovan Leech, and my own experiences guarding the pool for Tennessee Williams. It was built in 1929 as just a part of a 29-floor Medinah Athletic Club featuring a gym, a running

The pool at the Hotel InterContinental, built in 1929, still symbolizes the era.

track, an archery range, a bowling alley, two shooting galleries, and a boxing arena as well as ornate faux Egyptian ballrooms and lush guest rooms, all topped off with a port for dirigibles. Each meeting room, eating area, and lobby was designed in this grand Faux-Egyptian style.

The glory was short lived, however. In 1930, the Depression hit, ending the posh luxury of the Roaring '20s. During World War II the building was used to entertain troops as part of the USO. After the war it was converted to the Sheridan Hotel. It was as the Sheridan and later Raddison that I first saw Tennessee Williams at the pool. I had just graduated high school and was working as a lifeguard when the Pulitzer Prize–winning playwright scribbled "T Williams" in the guestbook. He wasn't the dashing, fedora-wearing, Hollywood figure of his heyday. A bit worse for wear after years of alcohol and prescription drug abuse, he was quite absent-minded, once forgetting to get dressed and walking naked into the elevator. But I will always remember those afternoons, sitting in white wicker chairs next to the blue water, listening to Mr. Williams talking about the glory days of Broadway with Jessica Tandy, or staying at the home of Paul Newman and Joanne Woodward while working on the movie adaptation of *Cat on A Hot Tin Roof*. When I knew him he was working on his final play, *A House Not Meant to Stand*, which, like most of his later works, took a beating from the critics. But, like the *Night of the Iguana's* Reverend T. Lawrence Shannon returning to the Pacific Ocean, Williams sought solace in the pool's tranquil blue waters from a world that was not always kind to strangers.

Capone's Country Distillery

It is a warm summer's night, but the breeze from the nearby creek and the old stone floor have a cooling effect on the customers who are enjoying "Dead Drop Spirits" at the Thornton Distillery. Distilled using water from an on-site artesian well, local distillers, as well as micro-breweries, have become the rage for a new generation of young drinkers. But what they do not know is that their custom is nothing new. Distilling and brewing are as much a part of Chicago history as Lake Michigan. Thornton's concentrates in one spot many of the elements of this history: Native Americans, John H. Kinzie, beer, German immigrants, and Al Capone. It is all there due to the artesian well that fed water from the nearby Thornton Creek. There is evidence, including signs of Indian fortification, arrowheads, and other tools of Native American occupation along the creek dating back to 1400. In 1833, John H. Kinzie and Gurdon Hubbard partnered to purchase the land. In 1836, a man named Don Carlos Berry opened what was to be the first of many breweries located near the Thornton Quarry, which until recently was the largest quarry in the world. In 1857, John Bielfedt, opened the brewery bearing his name.

The Artesian Well at the Thornton Distillery

In a few years, the I&M Canal was built nearby, as was a railroad. Along with the quarry workers, it was safe to say the brewery prospered. But that was not to last. In 1902, a flood damaged the brewery, followed by a tornado in 1904. In 1919, Prohibition meant the closure of the brewery. In 1920, it re-opened as a "soda pop" bottler owned by Carl Ebner Sr. But this, of course, was a front. Joe Saltis, an associate of Al Capone who knew the region, ran the brewery with the understanding that as long as it made money and Saltis handed it over, Saltis would be "safe." In the following years, Capone became Public Enemy #1 and Saltis #9. But by 1936, Capone was in jail, and Saltis was in hiding in Wisconsin. A succession of beers, including the Thornton Special, Four Crown Special Beer, Mc Avoy Malt Marrow, and White Bear Beer, flowed from the brewery. But around 1951, a succession of events forced the brewery to close. Over the years, the building housed a variety of businesses, including an auto repair shop. But in 2014, current co-owner Andrew Howell bought the land and the well, which had been dormant for over half a century. Howell began the long process of restoration of the site. Along with master distiller Ari Klafter, they went through the permit process and began distilling spirits using the well water, and today have revived the historic tradition of the brewery.

The Green Mill

If you want to go back into the era of jazz, gangsters, and fabulous cocktails, the Green Mill is a living museum and Chicago gem. Not only does it feature live jazz seven nights a week, but the entire structure, from the green neon sign to the bar and decorative statues, have been largely untouched by time. Located at 4802 N. Broadway and opened in 1907 as The Green Mill Gardens, it has seen performers like Louis Armstrong, Billie Holiday, Eddie Cantor, Al Jolson, and Sophie Tucker. It was also one of the many locations where Al Capone hung his hat, and a labyrinth of tunnels, running out from the basement underneath the nearby streets, still exists today. The lounge was owned for a time by Capone's top gunman, "Machine Gun Jack" Mc Gurn. It is said that Mc Gurn was given the club by Capone as a reward for his participation in the St. Valentines Day Massacre.

The club continued into the 1940s, '50s, and '60s, but during the 1970s and '80s, the suburban flight signaled hard times for the "Mill".

Historic Uptown

The Green Mill is just one of the entertainment spots that highlighted the glory days of Chicago's Uptown neighborhood. These include the **Uptown Theatre** at 4816 N. Broadway. When it was built, it was the second largest theater in the country behind Radio City Music Hall at 48,000 square feet. Entertainers from Bing Crosby and Duke Ellington to Frank Zappa and Bob Marley performed there. It has been vacant for many years, but funding is being made for its revival.

The **Aragon Ballroom** at 1106 W. Lawrence Ave. has seen the era of great big bands, boxing matches, a disco, and a roller rink. Another beautiful theater built in 1926, it still boasts the lavish accoutrements of the 1920s movie palaces.

The **Riviera Theater** at 4746 N. Racine Ave. is another holdover from the glory days of silent film. Built in 1917 and designed by Rapp and Rapp for the Balaban and Katz chain, it is now one of the centers for Chicago's hip-hop and alternative music scene.

In the 1980s, the club was purchased by Dave Jemilo, who recruited the top local jazz artists. Almost 50 years later, the club has become not only Chicago's most popular jazz club but a destination for tourists and a location for many films, including *Thief, Next of Kin, Prelude to a Kiss, High Fidelity,* and *Dreaming Grand Avenue.*

Wrigley Field

The great Cubs announcer Harry Caray used to say, "You can't beat fun at the old ballpark." Along with Boston's Fenway Park, Wrigley Field is "the old ballpark." Even during the colder months when the Cubs are not playing, Wrigley Field is still rated between the #3 and #5 tourist attraction depending upon the source. What is so amazing is that while every team save for the Red Sox has built a new stadium, Wrigley Field has not only survived but thrived. In recent years, a new hotel, shopping center, plaza, and dozens of bars, restaurants, and souvenir shops have turned the area into a top attraction. That is a far cry from the 1950s, '60s, and '70s. In the days of Ernie Banks, Ron Santo, and the "Bleacher Bums," Wrigley had an industrial train track running adjacent to the stadium and a few "old man's" bars, a doughnut shop, and Franksville, a sort of upscale hot dog stand.

In its earliest form, the stadium was named Weeghman Park after then-owner Charles Weeghman. The team was known as the Chicago Federals and later the Chicago Whales and played in the Federal League. In 1918, chewing gum magnate Phillip K. Wrigley bought the club. In 1926, he built an upper deck and renamed it Wrigley Field.

Those were glory days for the Chicago Cubs and Wrigley, as the team won National League Pennants in 1929, '32, '35, and '38. From 1921–1970, the Chicago Bears played at Wrigley, winning several championships on an oddly configured field. The Cubs, however, struggled for the next seven decades, not winning another Pennant until the 2016 World Series. By that time, the team had been bought by the Ricketts family, which began a $575 million renovation in 2013. This investment seems to have paid off, as Wrigley is now both a baseball and tourist mecca.

The Birthplace of Oz

The Wizard of Oz is the most watched film in American history. To this day, sayings like "There's no place like home" are part of the American idiom, crossing almost all generational, economic, and racial boundaries. Yet Dorothy, the Tin Man, the Scarecrow, the Cowardly Lion, and the Mighty Oz all started when a man named L. Frank Baum put a pen to paper in a clapboard wooden home on Chicago's north side. Baum and his family lived at 1667 N. Humboldt Blvd. from 1891 to 1910. In 1899, Baum wrote *The Wonderful Wizard of Oz*, which became a national bestseller, paving the way for 14 more Oz-themed books and eventually the classic film.

Reading Baum's life history, you can see some of the similarities between Baum and the mighty wizard. Born to a wealthy family, Baum nevertheless tried and failed at many professions before writing his first Oz book at the age of 40. He worked as a chicken farmer, actor, playwright, and dry-goods salesmen in South Dakota. Many say that his farm in South Dakota was the inspiration for the farm of Dorothy, one of the most famous characters in American film and literature. Failing at all, Baum, his wife, and four sons moved to Chicago in 1891, where he began working as a correspondent for the *Chicago Herald American*. Tiring of the rigors of journalism, he wrote his first children's books, *Mother Goose in Prose*, and *Father Goose*, which became bestsellers. This income allowed Baum to become a full-time writer, and an entire world came to life in this wooden home on a busy Chicago boulevard. Many say that the Emerald City was modeled after the gleaming "White City" of the Chicago World's Fair of 1893. Yet the word *Oz* came from a less inspirational source, as Baum once admitted that, stumped on a name for his magical kingdom, he looked at his file cabinet and saw a drawer marked O–Z. Baum eventually moved to California, where he bought land to create an Oz-themed amusement park and produced theatrical plays and silent films. Unfortunately, these projects were not successful, and Baum filed for bankruptcy in 1911.

The house was later torn down, and nine units of affordable rental housing now stand on the site. For many years, a wooden placard stood on the property, informing passersby of its significance. Yet the birthplace of this American icon needed to be celebrated. The property owner, Bickerdike Redevelopment, installed a yellow brick sidewalk in front of the property, and commissioned muralist Hector Duarte to create a 55-foot mosaic tile mural. Its theme—*there's no place like home.*

Monument to the birthplace of Oz at 1667 N. Humboldt Blvd.

Chaplin's Chicago Studio

The recent film *Babylon* introduced the subject of silent film to a generation, or many generations, who had little idea of the silent era. Most of the film takes place in Hollywood during the 1920s in what was then the wild mountains and desert of southern California as well as the mansions, swimming pools, and fancy cars that spawned the legend of "Hollywood." Yet few know that commercial silent film in America began in New York, and for a short time, Chicago was the center of America's film industry. It was the city where Charlie Chaplin made many of his first films, and stars like Gloria Swanson and Ben Turpin got their start.

It began with Broncho Billy Anderson. Born Maxwell Henry Aronson, from a Russian Jewish ancestry, he appeared in what many say was the first narrative film, *The Great Train Robbery*, in 1903. Now going under the name Bronco Billy Anderson, he and George Spoor founded Essanay studios in Chicago in 1907. A short comedy film, *The Hobo on Rollers*, allowed them to move to what was to become the landmark Essanay (a combination of their initials) Studios at 1333–45 W. Argyle St. in Chicago's Uptown neighborhood. They broke many barriers, including making the first screen versions of detective Sherlock Holmes, Charles Dickens's *A Christmas Carol*, and *The James Boys of Missouri*, the first of many films about the famous outlaw. These were not only artistic but technical triumphs that attracted the attention of the top stars, including the biggest star of the silent era, Charlie Chaplin.

In 1914, Chaplin signed on for a $10,000 bonus and arrived in Chicago with a contract to not only star in but have creative control of his projects. All in all, Chaplin made 14 films for Essanay, some in Chicago and others at the studios' western location in Niles, California, near San Francisco. Besides Chaplin, other players that worked at Essanay included Swanson and Turpin, who became stars, as well as lessor known names like Max Linder and John Rand. Locations like Foster Beach

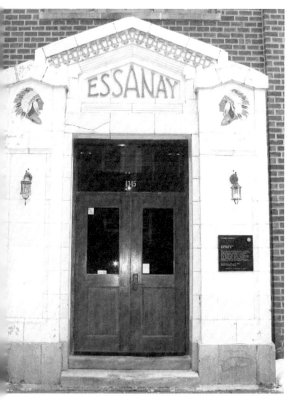

along Lake Michigan were used for beach and ocean scenes in adventure and pirate films, while Lincoln Park stood in for the jungle. For a time, Mack Sennett filmed his groundbreaking *Keystone Cops* comedies on the streets of Chicago.

This golden era, however, was short-lived. In 1916, Chaplin tired of Chicago's cold weather and dreary skies and headed to California. Anderson and Spoor continued to make films but was almost dormant by 1923. In later years, the studio was used by producer Norman Wilding to make industrial films through the 1970s. Today the building is listed on the National Register of Historic Places.

Walt Disney Was Born Here

Think of Mickey Mouse, Snow White, *Fantasia*, Donald Duck, Dumbo, and *The Lion King*—not to mention Disneyland, Walt Disney World, and the millions of people who visit these fantasy kingdoms from around the world every year. The name Disney is as American as baseball, and the delightful laughs and smiles of children and adults, not to mention billions of dollars, all trace back this small, wooden home. In 1881, Elias Disney bought property on Tripp and Palmer Aves. in Chicago. A carpenter, Disney and his wife Flora drew up architectural plans and built their home themselves beginning in 1883. In 1905, Walter Elias Disney, the youngest of four brothers, was born in this small, clapboard house.

The Disney family stayed in Chicago until Walter was four years old, then moved to Missouri. Like his youngest son, Elias Disney was somewhat of a dreamer, continually moving and starting new professions. Young Walt Disney returned to Chicago and as a freshman attended McKinley High School, (now the site of Chicago Bulls College Prep High School) and enrolled at the Art Institute of Chicago. World War I temporarily changed Disney's life, but in 1919, he returned to Kansas City and his brother Roy got him a job as a newspaper cartoonist. The rest, they say, is history. . . .

Over the years the small but handsome home, with its white picket fence and wooden front porch, was lived in by many families and updated with a basement and aluminum siding. The neighborhood has remained a stable, middle-class area, formerly the home of workers in the small, neighborhood factories. Into the 1980s and '90s, however, the home

Chicago birthplace of Walt Disney, 2156 N. Tripp Ave.

had fallen into disrepair. In 2013, Dina Benedon and Brent Young, two amusement-park designers, bought the home for $169,000 and began to restore it with a grant from the Disney Company and crowdsource funding.

"It really needed a lot of work. It didn't have this layout at all. We had to essentially take the entire house apart to see how it was put together originally," Young told ABC 30 Action News.

They restored the parlor and bedroom that Walt and his brother Roy lived in as young children and continued to bring the house back to its original look. The couple plans to build another addition to the home and open it as a museum. One question, however: With the billions that Disney Inc. makes every year, why does this couple still have to raise money?

It Used to Be the World's Largest Building

It was envisioned during the Roaring '20s, when Chicago's buildings and architecture were still establishing themselves as some of the greatest in the world. Financed by Marshall Field and Company and crafted in the Art Deco style, the Merchandise Mart spans almost two city blocks of some of the most prime real estate in the world. The building's construction required 29 million bricks; 40 miles of plumbing; 380 miles of wiring; nearly 4 million cubic yards of concrete; 200,000 cubic feet of stone; and 4,000 windows. Until the Pentagon was built in 1943, it was the largest building in the world; it had its own zip code. It was completed in May of 1930. Later that year, the economy crashed and the building did not experience the prosperity that was envisioned. In 1946, it was purchased by Joseph P. Kennedy, patriarch of the Kennedy dynasty. Some say Kennedy verbally agreed to donate the building to the University of Chicago for tax purposes, but since it was not on paper, he turned it into what was to become the main and lasting source of the Kennedy's income. Its importance to the Kennedy fortune was exemplified by the fact that it was managed by Sargent Shriver, the husband of Eunice Kennedy, and Chris Kennedy, the son of Robert F. Kennedy, until the building was sold to Vornado Realty in 1998. It has long been a hub for designers and furniture manufacturers worldwide. It is said that in the 1990s the Sultan of Brunei spent $1.6 million there in one week, furnishing his entire palace in one stop.

Some of its architectural highlights include the figures of 56 Native American chiefs circling the tower's crown, a frieze of 17 murals depicting the world of trade, and 8 statues and bronze busts that Joseph P. Kennedy commissioned to honor the giants of economics and trade, including Frank Woolworth, Marshall Field, Montgomery Ward, and Julius Rosenwald of Sears and Roebuck.

Today the Merchandise Mart continues to thrive both as a trade center and tourist attraction. Its many offices include high-end stores where one can purchase furniture, fireplaces, and especially high-end bathroom tubs, sinks, fixtures, and tile. There is a food court on the second floor where the public is allowed, but the upper floors are slated for professional designers and craftspeople and are largely off-limits to the general public. Yet the giant south wall, facing the Chicago River, has become the world's largest movie screen, as during warmer months artwork, dance performances, film, and music are projected on its walls, a 2.5 acre canvas the size of two football fields.

Chicago's Merchandise Mart

Chess Records, the Birthplace of Rock and Roll

There is a saying that "the blues had a baby and they called it rock and roll." Although the Delta South and Sun Records may have been the birthplace of rock music, Chicago's Chess Records served as its midwife, bringing blues music from the rural south to America's major cities. While at Chess, artists like Muddy Waters, Howlin' Wolf, Willie Dixon, Sonny Boy Williamson, and Little Walter transformed rural blues, which had been played on acoustic instruments, to the rhythm of Chicago's streets using amplification and a faster, harder beat. Or as The Rolling Stones harmonica player Sugar Blue told me, "They took a horse-drawn cart and turned it into a V-8 engine."

Chess was also instrumental in the formation of rock music. It was here that Leonard and Phil Chess first turned on the tape machine in front of Chuck Berry to first record songs like "Maybelline," "Roll Over Beethoven," "School Days," "Memphis, Tennessee," and "Johnny B. Goode." Rock and roll legend Bo Diddley released his classic rock hits "Bo Diddley" and "Who Do You Love?" at Chess Studios. Chess and its satellite labels

The Original Chess Studio

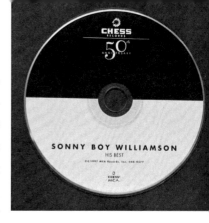

like Checker and Argo also crossed over into gospel, doo-wop, and soul music. Etta James's classic "At Last," was recorded at Chess Studios. So too was the doo-wop of the Moonglows and the Dells. If that was not enough, the label also recorded jazz artists like Sonny Stitt and Ahmad Jamal. As the legend of Chess Records grew, it spread across continents. So much so that when they first arrived in the United States, The Rolling Stones paid homage to the mecca by recording a single, "2120 S. Michigan," there. Other rock groups like Eric Clapton's The Yardbirds, Fleetwood Mac, and many more. Chess Records was also the subject of the 2008 film, *Cadillac Records*.

Keeping the Blues Alive

Today, Chess Studios lives on as part of The Blues Heaven Foundation. The building was purchased and refurbished by Willie Dixon, Chess artist and writer of songs such as "The Hoochie Coochie Man," "Whole Lotta Love," and hundreds more. The Blues Heaven Foundation hosts regular tours of Chess Studios, music clinics, and speaker series, as well as the Blues Heaven Garden "Music in the Garden" Concerts. Before his death, Dixon implored the younger blues fans and musicians to "keep the blues alive." Buddy Guy also recorded at Chess with Waters, Dixon, and many other artists. At 87 years old, Guy is the last living vestige of the golden age of Chicago blues, still playing and touring the nation and the world.

Grunge Rock Introduced Here

San Francisco has the Filmore, Los Angeles has the Troubadour, and Chicago has the Metro. While the first two venues were instrumental in establishing the San Francisco "hippie" sound of the late 1960s and the Troubadour helped spawn the singer-songwriter/California rock sound of the 1970s, the Metro was a key component in ushering in the alt rock/grunge sound of the 1990s. Opened in an old Swedish Hall in 1982 by entrepreneur Joe Shanahan, the venue's first breakthrough act was a Georgia "garage band" called R.E.M. During the club's first years, then-unknown bands like Metallica and Billy Idol also graced the stage. But as the 1980s ended, a new kind of music began to appeal to a new generation known as Generation X. In October of 1988, Chicago's own Smashing Pumpkins played their first major show and made their first live recording at the Metro. Through the years the band continued to call the Metro home, recording another live album there in 1993 and performing there throughout the years, including the 2022 reunion concert. In July of 1991, Pearl Jam appeared onstage at the club in one of their first major shows. Three months later, Nirvana took the stage at the Metro. Word of mouth from their concert on October 12, 1991, became part of what was to change rock for the rest of the decade. The list of alternative bands

Chicago's Cabaret Metro

who performed at the club is legendary, but Radiohead, the Foo Fighters, Soundgarden, Urge Overkill, and Jane's Addiction were just a few. But the Metro was always known for its open booking policy. Some of the artists who have played there include James Brown, Prince, Iggy Pop, The White Stripes, Weezer, The Bangles, Kanye West, Chance the Rapper, and The Black Crowes. Even Bob Dylan performed at the 1,000-plus-seat theater on its 50th anniversary, also in 1991.

In 2022, the club, now known simply as Metro, celebrated its 40th anniversary. Located on Chicago's north side between Wrigley Field and Graceland Cemetery, the club is adding its own chapter to Chicago's history.

Where Chicago's Rich and Famous Rest Forever

Perhaps it is only fitting, but the home of Chicago grunge was diagonally across from perhaps its most famous cemetery. Graceland Cemetery, at 4001 N. Clark St., was chartered in 1861. Some of the notable citizens buried there include: Marshall Field, founder of the great department store; Melville Fuller, Chief Justice of the Supreme Court; Jack Johnson, the first African American heavyweight boxing champion; Potter Palmer and Bertha Honoré Palmer, founders of the Palmer House Hotel; Alan Pinkerton, founder of the famed detective and security agency; Cyrus McCormick, inventor of the reaper; George Pullman, inventor of the Pullman railroad car; Charles Wacker, famous Chicago businessman and planner; and many more.

Chicago may be known as a hard-working city, but these places show us Chicagoans also know how to have fun.

SUPERBURGERS   THICK M

Chapter 4

Oddities and Curiosities: Monuments to Individualism in the Windy City

Sometimes individuals express themselves through becoming leaders. Others do it through the arts of music, writing, painting, and film. Yet others choose to bring out their identity and personality through building—but not always massive buildings with Romanesque columns, or gleaming spiraling skyscrapers. This chapter will celebrate the individuals and groups who have left their mark on Chicagoland through the odd, unusual, and oftentimes humorous things they have built. You will now read about how these structures gleam like diamonds of individuality that shine above the high-rises, row houses, and offices. What follow are monuments to the odd, unusual, and *fun*.

. . . .

Ancient Egypt on Clark St.

Walking down Clark St. in Lincoln Park, you see your usual condos, shops, and restaurants. Then suddenly you stop and see two larger-than-life statues of Ramses II surrounded by green terra-cotta palm fronds and brown terra-cotta lettering that reads: FIREPROOF. No, it is not a museum, but the former

headquarters of Reebie Moving and Storage. The building was designed and constructed after the discovery of King Tut's Tomb in 1922. At that time buildings ranging from hot dog stands to Grauman's Chinese Theater donned the Egyptian motif in what became a nationwide craze. Above the Ramses figures are women's heads wearing serpent hats embellished with lotus flowers, as well as winged disks, uraeus serpents, and winged scarabs, all of which are authentic reproductions of Egyptian sculpture. Due to these unique features, the building was placed on the National Register of Historic Places in 1979.

Children Feared "The Mummy"

Although the building is unique, it also presented a problem for many children growing up in the area. Many Chicagoans grew up with "Creature Features," which showed late night horror movies. The opening montage showed a mummy leaving a tomb that resembled the Reebie façade. Thus, many local children were afraid to pass by the building in fear that the Egyptian mummy would soon emerge.

Chicago's Fountain of Good and Evil

Every day people walk by thinking it is the "bird girl" from John Berendt's famous book, *Midnight in the Garden of Good and Evil*, but this little girl has a story all its own. During the late 19th century, people had few healthy options to quench their thirst. There were certainly no soft drinks, and the water often contained cholera and other diseases. So many turned to beer, ale, and hard cider—which were safer from germs but caused drunkenness. To help alleviate the problem, the Woman's Christian Temperance Union (WCTU) placed this fountain first at the site of the 1893 World's Fair and then in downtown Chicago. The hope was that "converted" drunks would not only find a place to quench their thirst but also find solace in the fountain.

After the WCTU office was closed, the fountain was first put into storage and then moved to Lincoln Park near an overpass to the north and the Chicago History Museum to the west. But in 1958 the statue was taken by thieves and lost to Chicagoans. In 2007, the Chicago Park District, along with groups from Lincoln Park and private owners, found the original plans and recast the statue. The little barefoot girl in her simple dress is now cast in bronze, holding out her hands to grasp a water bowl for pedestrians, joggers, bicycle riders, and the children from nearby Latin School.

The Castle Rising from the Plains

It looks like a tower on the Scottish plains. One even expects to see Macbeth standing on top of the turrets, spyglass in hand, watching the advancing army through Burnham Wood. Or perhaps a German baron overlooking his fiefdom, drinking out of a tankard glass and eating a freshly killed pheasant. There are no actual kings or barons in Chicagoland. Yet George Hofman, a local "beer baron" wanted a castle, so he built himself one. Located on a river and surrounded by tall prairie grass, especially to the west, it does indeed bear more than a passing resemblance to the Scottish Highlands or German plains. But about one quarter mile away are rows and rows of small suburban bungalows, a chain drugstore, and a pizza parlor, certainly not the barren plains of the Middle Ages. The Hofman Tower, located in Lyons/Riverside and near the Des Plaines River was built in 1908. Originally a power plant, it was the tallest local structure outside of the Chicago city limits. During its heyday, it had a picnic garden and hosted many weddings, parties, and other events. In addition to the tower, Hofmann built a concrete dam to create water deep enough for the fishing and recreational craft that utilized the park. The dam also generated the electricity that lit the streetlamps throughout the area. For a while, his plan worked. The area became a recreational spot for locals, with the rowboats and tower reminding many of the European nations that many of the settlers of the area came from. However, with the advent of the automobile, the locals began to travel to more distant and exotic spots for fishing and recreation. Also, the area became more industrial, and pollution from the factories made the Des Plaines River much less attractive for boating and swimming. The tower itself was closed as well.

Over the years, however, the building's stairs and upper floors deteriorated and became homes for birds and rodents. In the 1980s, it began to be restored and is now on the National Register of Historic Places. In recent years, many entrepreneurs have enquired about using the space as a brew pub. With its turrets and castle-like structure that can be seen for miles, it seems like a perfect fit.

The Hoffman Tower.
Photo by Jennifer Ann Stix

Geronimo Looms over Pulaski Ave.

During the 1960s and 1970s, the sight of massive pop-art fiberglass figures greeted drivers on streets and smaller highways across the country. From California to Maine, drivers and their families would encounter figures in the forms of hot dogs, hamburgers, cowboys, clowns, alligators, oranges, lobsters, and loons. Sinclair Service Stations had a dino-sized green brontosaurus munching on imaginary ferns from the roof. Bob's Big Boy had its trademark freckle-faced farm boy with his overalls and slicked-back cowlick. Chicago, however, has maintained its giant plastic, pop art statue. As you drive along Pulaski Ave. near 63rd St., amidst a mixture of small businesses, apartment complexes, and auto repair services,

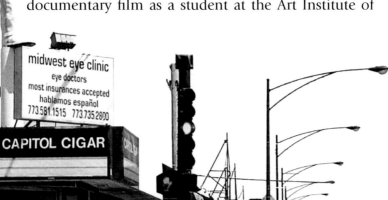

you'll see a giant, 45-foot-high statue of a Native American. Perched on top of the roof of Midwest Eye Clinic at 6254 S. Pulaski Rd., he greets passersby on foot, automobile, and CTA bus with his arm raised high, in a traditional Native American greeting.

Featured in the film *Wayne's World*," and *Playboy* magazine, it has long been the subject of local lore. "Apparently the previous owner collected Native American paraphernalia and saw this giant figure of Geronimo in Arizona," Don Lorincz, who made a documentary film as a student at the Art Institute of

Chicago on these giant statues stated. Lorincz also related how the owner had to bring back the statue in a flatbed truck which was an adventure in itself. Once the statue got to Chicago, he had to first get a special variance so as not to interfere with the flights coming from nearby Midway Airport. Once the statue was mounted on the roof, they found out its weight was too much and extra supports had to be added to the roof. When the figure was finally put in place, Chicago's high winds made it necessary to hold the statue steady with cables and wires.

Once Geronimo got there, he faced another hazard: practical jokers who continually shot arrows into the statue. At first the owner would pull out the arrows, but then he realized they attracted even more attention, so he would leave one or two in. Over the years, the cigar store went out of business, and the building was taken over by an eye clinic. Yet the statue was such a landmark the new owner simply hung a giant sign around Geronimo's neck. In keeping with the statue's kitschy humor, Geronimo now has a pair of black glasses and wears a sign that says, "EYE Can See Now." In an area with few notable landmarks, large stores, or structures, this once-odd eyesore has become a source of neighborhood pride.

Chicago's Grease Drive-In

You drive into a slotted spot bathed in Americana neon light, then look at the menu, which is on a post next to the car. You make your selection—the "Superdawg," a Chicago hot dog covered with a hard dill pickle, onions, sport peppers, and the trademark bright green relish. When you press the button, you give your order through a speaker. But unlike the common drive-thru, your food is brought to you by a "carhop," sometimes on roller skates, who attaches a tray to your half-rolled-down window to the sound of Dion singing "Runaround Sue."

If this sounds like a scene from the movie *Grease*, you are not wrong. In fact, the very spot you are dining in was often frequented by Jim Jacobs, a neighborhood resident who wrote the classic play, inspired in part by his visits to the classic Chicago drive-in.

Located at 6363 N. Milwaukee Ave., Superdawg recently celebrated its 75th Anniversary. The restaurant was started in 1948 by Maurie Berman, a returning GI studying to be a CPA at Northwestern University, and his wife Flaurie, a public school teacher. At first, it was a side job for the summers, but as business expanded, the couple decided to make it a full-time venture. In order to attract attention, they decided to erect a "statue" of sorts. In the pre-website era during the 1940s and '50s, America's roadsides were filled with giant plastic or fiberglass figures to attract the attention of drivers on the highway. The Bermans wanted to have the entire restaurant shaped like a hot dog on a bun, but that was too expensive. So they settled on two hot dogs, one representing the male, muscle-flexing Maurie, and the other the adoring female (remember this was the 1950s) gazing at him. Over the years, "Maurie and Flaurie" have become not only a symbol of the stand but a neighborhood landmark and source of pride.

The name "Superdawg" was also a product of Berman's creativity. Hoping to cash in on the Superman comic book craze, they named it after the man of steel. Before the electronic speaker system was installed, customers also signaled it was time to order by flashing their headlights.

As the new Millennium approached, Superdawg began attracting national attention on shows like *The Hot Dog Program*, in the *New York Times*, and *1,000 Places to See in the United States Before You Die*. In 2009 a second location was added to the North at 333 S. Milwaukee Ave. in Wheeling, Illinois. Maurie Berman passed away in 2015, and Flaurie in 2018, but both restaurants are now run by members of the Berman family, who are keeping the *Grease* tradition alive.

The Last 1893 World's Fair Ticket Booth

It was the party that turned Chicago from a large Midwestern town into a world-class city. In an era before airplanes and automobiles, an estimated 27 million people came to the fair from literally every corner of the world during its six-month run. Gazing across what was called the Midway Pleasance, visitors saw over 700 newly built Romanesque buildings connected by a series of lagoons and canals as if Venice and ancient Rome were combined into one entity. There were Egyptian pyramids, Chinese and Japanese villages, artwork from ancient Greece and Rome, music by John Phillip Sousa and a pipe organ with 39,000 pipes, dramas, demonstrations of cooking and culture, and dancers (including the now-infamous "hoochie koochie dancers"). The fair was an artistic and visual extravaganza.

A unique remnant from the 1893 World's Fair

Technologically, the fair changed not only Chicago but the world, leading the way into the 20th century. Electricity was first used on a large scale at the fair, lighting the entire area like magic and even lighting the first nighttime football game. Other groundbreaking inventions introduced at the fair include Thomas Edison's kinescope, the telephone switchboard, the first voice recording, the moving sidewalk, and the first mechanical dishwasher. On the "fun" side, the fair saw the introduction of the zipper, the Ferris wheel, and Wrigley's Gum, and the hot dog and hamburger were first sold en masse at the fair. During its proceedings, the man many call America's first serial killer, H. H. Holmes, also lured unsuspecting visitors, mainly young women, into his nearby home which was turned into a maze of murder. These events are intertwined with the work of architect Daniel Burnham in Erik Larson's book, *The Devil in the White City*.

Only Memories and Photos Remain

After the fair however, a massive fire destroyed many of the buildings constructed for the fair. Others deteriorated over the years and were moved or torn down. Today, the only surviving structure from the Fair is the former Palace of Fine Arts, which now houses Chicago's Museum of Science and Industry, the largest science museum in the Western Hemisphere. Besides a replica of the golden Statue of the Republic, there is also one original structure left in its entirety from the fair. Sitting on the grounds of Oak Park's Hill's DeCaro House (designed by Frank Lloyd Wright) is a small, white box with tiny Romanesque columns, barred windows, and two planters. Almost 150 years ago, millions of people—ladies in bustles and fine hats and men in tuxedos—walked past this structure. Now it sits almost unnoticed, save for a wonderful yellow Labrador retriever who greets visitors from the house next door.

Route 66 Begins Here

"It winds from Chicago to LA." For generations, drivers, history buffs, and musicians from songwriter Bobby Troupe to Nat King Cole and The Rolling Stones have been "getting their kicks, on Route 66." But while the legendary cross-country mother road conjures up visions of winding through small Midwestern hamlets (Joplin, Missouri), desert interspersed with small towns (Flagstaff, Kingman, Barstow), and crazy

teepee motels, car graveyards, diners, and gift shops in between, it actually starts in one of the most urban sections of America. The corner of Michigan and Adams, where the sign says the road begins, is kitty-corner from Chicago's Art Institute and its famous lions. Also nearby are the legendary Chicago Athletic Club, the Auditorium Theater, and Lou Mitchell's Restaurant. Opened in 1923, Lou Mitchell's Restaurant a few blocks east at 565 W. Jackson Blvd. was one of the first businesses to cater to the route's truck drivers at the beginning of a journey with their breakfast skillets filled with pancakes, eggs, bacon, sausage, corned beef hash,

and coffee. Traveling further southwest off I-55 in Willowbrook, Illinois, is another former Route 66 treasure, the Dell Rhea Chicken Basket. The restaurant started as a gas station along Route 66. As the many cars and trucks stopped to get their vehicles repaired, the drivers stated that they could use a bite to eat before the long trip. Two local women suggested they could fry up some of their chickens. Fried chicken, wrapped in a napkin, can stay fresh for a while, and the recipe became so popular the station owner partnered with the women and turned the service station into a restaurant. Purchased by Dell Rhea, it became so popular that a bus depot was opened nearby. During the winter months, the owner came up with another idea to attract customers—flooding the roof using sill cocks that gushed out water. He installed railings and a spotlight, turning the roof into an outdoor skating rink. Today, the Dell Rhea Chicken Basket, with its gleaming original neon sign that reads "Dell Rhea Chicken Basket, Cocktail Lounge," is another local celebrating Route 66 and its history. The road continued to run for a total length of 2,448 miles. After its starting point in Chicago, it runs southwest through Illinois, Missouri, Kansas, Oklahoma, Texas, and Arizona, ending at the Pacific Ocean in Santa Monica, California. While large interstate highways have replaced what John Steinbeck called "the Mother Road," for general transportation, much of the highway has been restored and it is still a destination for tourists from around the world.

A Thirsty Newsboy Makes Good

The Rosenberg Fountain was built and erected around the time of the Columbian Exposition. The fountain was financed by Joseph Rosenberg, who grew up in Chicago. As a poor immigrant who delivered newspapers, he was seldom able to

get even a cup of cold water on his route. He vowed that if he ever became wealthy, he would create a fountain where newsboys and other poor workers could get a drink on a hot day. He later moved to San Francisco and made a fortune but did not forget his struggles as a poor child. Upon his death he left a $10,000 bequest for a fountain to be erected near his childhood home. The South Park Commissioners accepted the donation and installed the monument on the southwest end of

Grant Park on S. Michigan Ave. The original statue was a nude depiction of Hebe, the voluptuous goddess of youth and cup bearer to the gods. Religious and temperance groups protested, and Hebe was given a robe that covered all but one breast. The statue was designed by Chicago architects Bauer and Hill. Passersby are no longer encouraged to drink from the fountain, but they can still listen to the gentle trickle of the water as it is sent skyward, with gravity pulling it back to its cement base. This action also sets off a misty spray, and many pedestrians stand near the fountain on hot summer days hoping to cool themselves with the mist.

The "School of Beer"

If you have ever enjoyed a Budweiser, Pabst, Coors, Busch, Goose Island, or many craft beers, your beverage's recipe and taste have a history at the Siebel Institute of Brewing Technology. Born in Dusseldorf, Germany, in 1845, John E. Siebel earned a PhD in Physics and Chemistry from the University of Berlin before moving to Chicago in 1866. Two years later, he opened John E. Siebel's Chemical Laboratory.

"The city was a more open market, but Siebel didn't want to just brew," John Hannafan, Director of Education at the Siebel Institute says. "He had the idea of training brewers in the German style of brewing. That is where he found his niche."

In 1872, Siebel opened a facility on Belden Ave. and changed the school's name to the Siebel Institute of Technology. Besides running classes on yeast, wort production, ice and refrigeration, quality control, and bottling, he wrote over 200 books and articles on beer and brewing. Siebel soon became the go-to expert on brewing, and Chicago the go-to city for brewing education. "During the late 1800s and early 1900s, J. E. Siebel trained hundreds of brewers, many with familiar names like Pabst, Busch, and Coors," Hannafan says.

Courses were conducted in English and German, and by 1907, there were five regular courses, including a six-month brewer's course, a two-month post graduate course, a three-month engineer's course, a two-month master's course, and a two-month bottler's course.

Irony and coincidence abound in our world, but perhaps there is no better example than Dr. J. E. Siebel dying on December 20, 1919, 27 days before the onset of Prohibition. The Institute

Chicagoans love their beer.

survived the period by offering courses in yeast and baking, carbonated beverages, and refrigeration. By then, the facility had moved north to Pulaski and Peterson Aves. His sons F. P. Siebel, Sr., and F. P.'s sons Fred and Ray moved into a new era. A fourth generation, Ron and Bill Siebel, began working at the Institute in the 1960s. For a short period the school was located at 1777 N. Clybourn Ave., in the back room of the Goose Island Brewery. In 2013, the Siebel Institute moved to 900 N. Branch St., in the same building as the Kendall College. Today it is in its own facility at 322 S. Green St. Almost 150 years after a young German immigrant took portions of yeast, hops, and other grains by horse-drawn wagon to make beer, the Siebel Institute is training a new generation of brewers and micro-brewers who travel from around the world to learn the art of brewing.

The World's Oldest Barbershop

Established in 1805 in Mayfair, London, England, it is the world's oldest barbershop according to the *Guinness Book of World Records*. It has served Dukes and members of England's aristocracy, including members of the royal family since King George III. The words "by royal appointment" are often used in connection with Truefitt & Hill Barbershop. British leaders including Sir Winston Churchill, Field General George Montgomery, and William Gladstone have received the shop's services. Notable authors and celebrities including Charles Dickens, William M. Thackeray, Lord Byron, Oscar Wilde, Beau Brummell, Alfred Hitchcock, and Laurence Olivier, as well as Americans John Wayne, Danny Kaye, Frank Sinatra, Fred Astaire, and Cary Grant have also sat in the plush leather chairs. The Chicago branch is neither as old nor as storied as its London counterpart, but it still carries on the Truefitt & Hill tradition. Paneled in 120-year-old Mahogany, the décor is old English gentleman, with pictures of racehorses and

hunting dogs and scenes from the royal fox hunt on the walls. In addition, Truefitt & Hill has locations in Toronto, Beijing, Canberra, Sydney, Dhaka, India, Kuala Lumpur, Singapore, Kuwait, Bangkok, Nepal, Sri Lanka, Bhutan, Vietnam, Myanmar, Bangladesh, and Prague. Services include old-fashioned, hand-heated leather straight razor shaves, haircuts, manicures, and massages, all for gentlemen. Formerly in the John Hancock Building, the shop is now located on Wells St. in Chicago's Old Town neighborhood. While the treatment, surroundings, and history may be regal, the price, at $60 for a "royal haircut and shampoo" is less than many would pay at higher-end salons in Chicago.

Home of the Hippies

Truefitt & Hill is located on the edge of Chicago's Old Town neighborhood. Established in the 1880s, it was the home of German immigrants Oscar Mayer and Dr. Scholl (yes, they were real people). Located in the 43rd Ward, it was ruled for decades by Alderman Paddy Bauler. Weighing in at over 300 pounds, the saloonkeeper/alderman is famous for his quote, "Chicago ain't ready for reform." During the 1960s, it became Chicago's hippie hangout, as jazz clubs featured Miles Davis, and the burgeoning folk and rock scene saw performers ranging from Bob Dylan and Pete Seeger to Janis Joplin and Led Zeppelin. The music led to a counterculture explosion. Hare Krishnas wandered the streets in orange robes burning incense, and head shops like Bizarre Bazaar was a mall in itself selling bongs, rolling papers, black-light posters, and psychedelic lights. Attractions like Ripley's Believe It or Not Museum and the Royal London Wax Museum brought tourists. Today, the neighborhood has shed its hippie past to become an upscale residential and shopping area.

The Orange Garden Sign, the Neon Sign That Will Live in History

The glowing neon sign reads CHOP SUEY in neon green while CHOW MEIN flashes underneath. In the 1930s, '40s, and '50s, placards like this were a part of almost every major city. They glowed and flashed in the night, and you would almost expect to see Humphrey Bogart walking under one, lighting a cigarette. Chop Suey houses, with neon signs hanging over the sidewalk, have been part of the American landscape since the dish was invented by Chinese-American cooks.

The sign that adorned the Orange Garden had been glowing in Chicago's North Center neighborhood since the 1930s. The restaurant itself opened in 1932, serving traditional Cantonese/American dishes like egg fu young, egg rolls, and of course chop suey and chow mien. Through the years it endured, and when Chinatown's Wan Kow closed in 2018, the Orange Garden became Chicago's oldest Chinese restaurant. In early 2022, the business was taken over by new owners who, perhaps due to the expense of repair, no longer wanted the sign. On April 30, 2022, the orange neon "artwork" went up for sale as part of a Chicago memorabilia auction. The story has it that years ago, Smashing Pumpkins front man and lifetime Chicagoan Billy Corgan told his partner Chloe Mendel that he loved the sign. Mendel remembered their conversation, and when she saw it up for sale on social media, she put in a bid for $17,000. The sign now lives on as part of Madame Zuzu's, Corgan's tea and used record store in Highland Park, Illinois.

The Morrie Mages Handprint Wall

Compared to Boston, New York, and Los Angeles, Chicago's major sports teams boast few championships. But the city has still had more than its share of great athletes—some may argue the greatest. In recent years, they have been memorialized by statues in front of the United Center, Wrigley Field, Soldier Field, and Guaranteed Rate Field. But before the new millennium, Chicago's greatest public memorial to its sports legends was the series of handprints pressed into the concrete walls surrounding the former Morrie Mages Sporting Goods Store. People of a certain age will remember this building at La Salle and Ontario as the former site of a six-story emporium that billed itself as "the world's largest sporting goods store." As at the sidewalk of Grauman's Chinese Theatre in Los Angeles, the handprints of many legends are pressed into the wall along with their names etched into the wet concrete. From the giant paws of former coach Mike Ditka to other Bears legends like Jim McMahon, Mike Singletary, and Walter Payton; the Cubs's Andre Dawson, Sammy Sosa, Ron Santo, Harry Caray, and Ryne Sandberg; White Sox's Minnie Miñoso, Billy Pierce, and Frank Thomas; Blackhawks's Stan Mikita, Denis Savard, and Bobby Hull; Bulls's Michael Jordan, John Paxson, and Johnny "Red" Kerr; boxer Tony Zale; and many more. Converted into The Sports Authority in the 1990s, the building is under proposed development. Let's just hope they find a way to save that wall.

The "Bob Newhart Building"

For six years, millions of Americans tuned into CBS to see the ordinary everyman "Bob Hartley," the balding, middle-aged psychiatrist, leave his downtown office, board an "El" train, then emerge to enter a high-rise building on Chicago's lakefront. That building, Thorndale North Beach Tower at 5490 N. Sheridan Rd., has finally been recognized as the television home of Bob Newhart, perhaps Chicago's most popular sitcom star.

Robert Newhart was born in 1929 in Oak Park, Illinois. He attended St. Ignatius College Prep High School and Loyola University in Chicago. Working as a copywriter at the old Fred Niles Studio (now the site of Oprah Winfrey's studio), he began making humorous "one way" phone calls, the most memorable of which may have been Sir Walter Raleigh reporting back to pre-colonial England. They were turned into comedy albums that became hits, and an entertainment career spanning over 50 years followed. *The Bob Newhart Show* ran on CBS from 1972

Now Chicago Is a Television Star

At the time of the filming of *The Bob Newhart Show*, there had been no TV shows filmed in Chicago save for another brief opening shot of the Cabrini-Green projects for the show *Good Times*. So, when large cameras hit the streets, it was an event. Currently, Chicago is experiencing a boom in TV production. Shows like *Chicago PD* and *Chicago Fire* have used Chicago's streets and gritty landscape as a backdrop for over a decade. *Chicago Med*, *The Bear*, and many others use Chicago as their home. Now, like in LA, Chicagoans simply walk past television production sets, and drivers complain that they are holding up traffic.

to 1976. Not only did he live in and "enter" the building, but Chicagoans have noted the circuitous "TV" route he took there, from the Loop to Evanston, and then back to the Lake Shore. While appearing on the Conan O'Brien show in 2021, Newhart himself joked, "The 'L' at some point goes on the ground, which is about 55 blocks from our apartment. I did this every day. I miss my stop and walk back 55 blocks to our apartment. Now, would you want a therapist who missed his stop every day?"

In September of 2022, the Edgewater Historical Society placed a plaque commemorating the site in front of the building at Lane Beach near Sheridan and Thorndale Ave. The Edgewater Historical Society had been working for years to get the site recognized, and finally put up a placard across the street.

"We had to do something to acknowledge Newhart's impact on Edgewater," John Holden, President of the Society said. "This is the one spot in Edgewater that was routinely seen by tens of millions of TV watchers for years."

So now, when you walk by and say to yourself, "Hmm, that building looks familiar," you know why.

The TV home of Bob Newhart
on Chicago's lakefront

The Beatles, The Rolling Stones, and Al Capone Ate Here

Question: What do The Beatles, Al Capone, and The Rolling Stones have in common? They all sampled ice cream treats at Margie's Candies. Located in Chicago's Wicker Park neighborhood, the business has been operating since 1921. In this period that spans more than a century, the area has remained staunchly working class, changing somewhat from Greek to German to Polish, Hispanic, and now hosts a mixture of people, including a new generation of bicycle-riding, tattooed "hipsters." Yet the standards of dress and transportation were quite different when the store opened in 1921 at 1960 N. Western Ave. The first owner was a Greek immigrant named Peter George Poulos, who turned it over to his son George. During this era, Al Capone, a not-so-sweet guy, who appeared to have a sweet tooth, would send a driver to fetch ice cream treats. Originally named the Security Sweet Shop, the younger Poulos met and married a woman named Margie and re-christened the business in her honor in 1933. Margie added her homemade candies to the store's array of treats and ran the business while her husband was serving in World War II and after her husband died in 1954.

As America moved into the rock and roll era, Margie's served as a classic example of the American "soda shop." Adorned with traditional "ice cream chairs," small tables, a soda fountain, and decorations including dolls and pennants. One may expect Veronica and Jughead of the Archies to be sitting at the table, but Margie's did one better. In 1964, after The Beatles had played a concert at Chicago's Comiskey Park, they arrived at Margie's with four women and indulged in banana splits, a far cry from the LSD and other drugs they admitted to taking a short time later. Today, Margie's has a case of Beatles's memorabilia, including albums, posters, and photos they signed between spoonsful of banana and fudge. Margie was an older woman at the time of the visit, so it was probably a younger employee who recognized the rock stars. This may be evidenced by Margie claiming that The Beatles returned a year later, except there were five of them. Once again, a former employee informed her that those were probably The Rolling Stones. In the early 1990s Margie became a rock star herself, appearing on MTV several times. In 1993, Liz Phair also posed for photos at Margie's for a story featured in *Newsweek*.

Margie died in 1995, and her son Peter took over the business. He continued the tradition and even opened a second location at 1813 W. Montrose Ave. In May of 2023, Peter George Poulos died at the age of 86. Today, Peter's son George still runs the business, representing the fourth generation of the Poulos family at Margie's.

Margie's Candies has served The Beatles, The Rolling Stones, and Al Capone.

Route 66's Gemini Giant

Before the internet and mass media, business had to figure out creative ways to attract customers. This giant green spaceman, standing 28 feet tall, definitely did so for the Launching Pad Drive-In. Located on Route 66 southwest of Chicago, this statue has greeted visitors and diners since the early 1960s, when John and Bonnie Korlic converted a smaller hot dog stand into the Launching Pad. The statue was originally a "muffler man," but the couple had it painted green, gave it a helmet and rocket, and named it the Gemini Man. Remember, the '60s was the decade Americans landed on the moon, and the Gemini spaceship started it all. For many years this oversized astronaut greeted families as they made their way down America's mother road. It isn't hard to imagine a carload traveling in a "woody" station wagon on a hot summer day. The children would scream, "Mommy, daddy, look at the big spaceman." The father would shake his head, thinking about the long drive ahead, perhaps a bit intrigued. The children would continue pleading until finally mom would chime in, "honey, maybe you should stop there. It is awfully hot. And they have ice cream. Besides, that big guy is kind of interesting. I wonder if anybody who works there can tell us where it came from?" Yet as new highways were built bypassing Route 66, fewer and fewer "woody wagons" visited, and the restaurant was closed in 2010. In 2017, Holly Barker and Tully Garret bought the Launching Pad. The reborn restaurant was a true-to-form, old-style roadside restaurant, whose offerings include the Gemini Dog, the Rocket Burger, shakes, chicken, fries, and ice cream, with a nod toward both Chicago (Chicago dog, Italian beef) and the Carolinas (slaw dog, slaw burger). The restaurant, however, did not reopen in the spring of 2023 and the website states that it is temporarily closed. The statue still stands and there are plans to turn the building into a Route 66 Visitors Center.

The Old Stone Jail Cell

All was not always fun and adventure on Route 66. Sometimes things got out of hand and folks had to go to jail. Such was the case in Gardener, Illinois, which is located along the old Route 66 not far from the Launching Pad. In 1906, the town built a small, two-room structure with two cells and a section for the guards. There was no toilet—only a bucket. The small jail cell, made out of local limestone with a tiled roof and brick chimney, housed criminals until 1950. Today it is open as a tiny, free museum, and anyone passing through the area can sit in the tiny, cave-like cell.

Butchers and meat cutters at the former Gepperth's Market, circa 1906, are just one example of how Chicago's many ethnic groups shaped the city's food and culture. Photo courtesy of Gepperth's Market

Chapter 5

Chicago's Ethnic Melting Pot

They came first on ships, crossing oceans and enduring storms, bad food, and most of all, fear. Fear of leaving home. Fear of never seeing loved ones again. Fear of not having money or knowing the language. Yet for many, the first thing they saw was the Statue of Liberty. Lifelong Americans struggle to pass it without tears welling in their eyes. You can only imagine the emotions of someone from a new land seeing this symbol of freedom. From there they went by wagon, carriage, and later train and automobile, crossing half of America until they arrived in Chicago. And arrive they did: Germans, Irish, Poles, Lithuanians, Swedes, Italians, Norwegians, Greeks, Chinese, and later Mexicans, Puerto Ricans, African Americans from the South, and others from many more nations. They arrived to find not gold-paved streets but slum-like hovels. They worked in the stockyards. They built the railroads, the I&M Canal, and rebuilt a city devastated by fire. But along with this they brought their magnificent cultures—food, music, arts, and craftsmanship. They produced great churches and buildings, along with beer and foods like deep-dish pizza, Italian beef, and saganaki to name a few. In this way, they forged what was to become the great tapestry that is Chicago.

. . . .

City of Beer: The Schoenhofen Brewery Historical District

The first immigrant group to arrive in large numbers in Chicago were the Germans. Many came in the early 1850s, after the German Revolution of 1848 to 1849. The immigrants, known as "48ers," brought with them many elements of German culture, including their craftmanship, religion, and especially architecture, as many of the Germans who arrived in Chicago were skilled craftsmen who helped to build the city's churches and civic structures. But many think their greatest contribution was lager beer. It is estimated that in 1900 there were 60 breweries in Chicago producing 100 million gallons of beer a year, and a majority of those

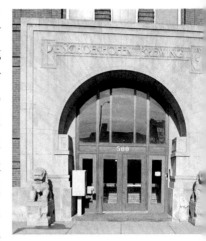

The grand entrance

breweries were German run. The Schoenhofen Brewery complex was the largest of these, producing 190,000 gallons a year by 1900. The Schoenhofen building may be the oldest brick structure in Chicago. There is a date of 1867 etched into the cornice, but that was merely the year Schoenhofen took over the structure. One of the keys to Schoenhofen was an underground, artesian well 1,600 feet beneath the property. It provided a virtually unlimited supply of spring water and is still in existence today, capable of producing over a million gallons of water a year for the next 100 years. The company shut down during Prohibition but reopened in 1933, still making the popular Edelweiss. In the 1940s, Atlas Brewing purchased it and in the 1950s it became part of Drewrys, a popular beer label based in South Bend, Indiana.

Two buildings remain, including the brick-and-cement archway that reads "Schoenhofen Brewery." On the cornice of the administration building is a six-pointed star. While many think this hexagram is the Star of David, it is actually the "Bierstern," a German symbol of brewing purity that dates back to the 1300s. The ornate Victorian designs of architect Adolph Cudell, (administration building) and Schmidt, Garden, and Martin (powerhouse) are now forever protected as part of the National Register of Historic Places. Of course, beer and brewing are just one example of the German contribution to Chicago's culture. Into the 1970s, German restaurants and beer gardens filled Chicagoland, especially the north side. Many settled in the Lake View and North Center areas. The restaurant Zum Deutchen Eck at Lincoln and Southport took up almost an entire city block. There is still a small concentration of German restaurants and culture in the Lincoln, Western, and Irving areas. They are centered around The Dank Haus German Cultural Center, which offers classes in German language, music and cultural performances, and a library of German language books.

The former Schoenhofen Brewery is now a landmark.

Old Saint Patrick's Church

Through Mayors Richard J. and Richard M. Daley, who stood watch over Chicago for over half a century, through the many members of the police force, business community, and clergy, the Irish have had a major impact on Chicagoland. First arriving in the 1830s, Irish immigrants began coming to Chicago after the Potato Famine of 1845. According to the Encyclopedia of Chicago, there were over 300,000 people of Irish decent living in Chicago in 1890. And unlike some immigrant groups, the Irish journey to Chicago continued throughout the 20th century, with an estimated 36,000 Irish arriving during the 1980s. Many Irish settled in the areas still called Bridgeport or Back of the Yards. Bridgeport was known for its local Irish residents who often grew cabbage in their gardens and empty fields. The Irish worked as tradesmen, bar and saloon owners, and also bore generations of Chicago policemen and women. Upon gaining financial stability, many Chicagoans of Irish origin also moved to the Beverly neighborhood on Chicago's far south side as well as to nearby suburbs like Oak Lawn.

Besides politics, the greatest Irish contribution to Chicago culture may be the Catholic parishes. Chicagoland is still filled with churches, hospitals, orphanages, schools, and universities like Loyola and De Paul that were built in part due to the Irish Catholic influence. But the greatest standing monument to Chicago's Irish and Gaelic community may be Old Saint Patrick's Church. Dedicated in 1856, it was named after St. Patrick, the Apostle of Ireland. Taking up an entire city block just northwest of downtown, the church boasts two octagonal spires, as well as 15 stained glass windows that tell the story of the Bible. It was originally an Irish parish and had a neighborhood school, St. Patrick's—Chicago's oldest school, which has since moved to a larger location near Belmont and Austin. Yet as the Irish moved away to neighborhoods like Beverly, and with the building of the Kennedy Expressway, the area was left with few parishioners. To combat this, Father John Wall, pastor of the church, looked at the languishing parish and its finances. Wall saw in second- and third-generation Irish a need to return to their roots and the social structure the church provided. In 1985, he organized the "World's Largest Block Party," which helped to revitalize the parish. The church has also hosted Irish music festivals combining local and Irish musicians and broadcast nationally on PBS. In 2021, the church, now on the National Register of Historic Places, celebrated 175 years of faith.

The Greeks Light Up the Town

The scene: almost any Greek restaurant in Chicago. Families, groups of coworkers, and couples are all sitting and socializing. Suddenly a server stands next to the table and raises a metal pan filled with kasseri cheese. The cheese is quickly doused with brandy and the server flicks a lighter crying "Opaaa!" There is a burst of flame. There is generally a whoosh of Oohs and Ahs, followed by clapping. The tray is then doused with a burst of fresh squeezed lemon. The flames subside, and the server lowers a tray of saganaki.

Chicago has a special claim to the dish. While in Greece the cheese is usually baked in a pan, Chicago's version is served with the circus-like flashing flame. In 1968, Chris Liakouras,

Flaming Saganaki, a Chicago invention

the owner of Chicago's now-closed Parthenon Restaurant, is largely credited with the dramatic burst of fire accompanied by the shouting of "Opaa." Trying to promote Greektown, Liakouras realized that many non-Greeks expected something unique and lively from a Greek-inspired room, and in response he came up with the flaming cheese. Since then, flaming saganaki has become a trademark in Chicago's Greektown and a symbol for Greeks in Chicagoland.

Although not as numerous or influential as the Germans, Irish, Italians, or Poles, Greeks were a major immigrant group, adding to Chicago's population. Greeks started arriving in large groups after the turn of the 20th century. By 1930, almost 30,000 Greeks had settled in the area called "The Delta," around Jane Addams Center along Halsted St. As the Greeks became more prosperous, they moved north toward downtown, centering on Jackson and Halsted Sts.

After World War II, Greeks began moving north, establishing communities near Lawrence and Western Aves. and in suburbs like Morton Grove to the north and Palos Heights to the south.

Chicago's Greektown
The Best Greek Food in America

Although fewer Greeks now live in the area, Chicago's Greektown has one of the largest concentrations of Greek restaurants outside of Greece. Major restaurants include The Greek Islands, at 700 S. Halsted St.; Athena, at 212 S. Halsted St.; Nine Muses Bar and Grill, at 315 S. Halsted St.; The Zeus Restaurant, at 806 W. Jackson St. (across the street from Athenian Candle). There are also the Artopolis Bakery at 306 S. Halsted St. and the Hellenic Museum at 333 S. Halsted St., which celebrates the culture and contributions of Greek Americans throughout the nation. In addition, there is Athenian Candle. Established in 1921, Athenian Candle was one of the first major businesses in the area. While people do not use candles for light anymore, candles are a very important part of the Greek Orthodox religion. Other items sold at Athenian Candle include Greek cookbooks, Greek and American flags, worry beads (komboloi), key chains, magnets, and signs that say, "Parking for Greeks Only."

The Pui Tak Center/ On Leong Building

The Chinatowns in New York and San Francisco may be larger, but neither of them has a structure as grand as this. Begun in 1926 and finished in 1928, it contains two pagoda towers and a line of open third-floor balconies and is adorned from top to bottom with exquisite terra-cotta dragons, jade green lions, and ornate carvings. Taking up two city blocks, the building looks like an emperor's palace and has long been the physical and symbolic headquarters of Chicago's Chinese American community.

Through the years, the building has served as an immigrant assistance center, a restaurant and gift shops a shrine, a Catholic grade school, and a performance and meeting center, and it now hosts classes in English for new generations of Chinese immigrants. The structure is also known for a somewhat shady past. It was formerly the headquarters of the On Leong Merchants, a group that was known as a gang or "Tong" that controlled gambling and vice within the Chinatown community.

In 1988, however, the building was seized by the FBI, which had found elaborate gambling apparatus inside.

In the following years, groups including the Chinese Christian Union Church, Partners in Preservation, and other community organizations have reopened and restored the building to its former status as a community center. In 2007, it was named a Chicago Landmark, receiving more votes than 24 other historic sites.

The Chicago Tamale

Much of Chicago's ethnic street food follows the same "recipe." Start with the base of an old ethnic or folk dish, add local ingredients, and make it more portable with the ability to be produced more quickly and at a lower cost. There is no greater example of this than the "Chicago Tamale." The Central American version of meat, masa, and sauce wrapped in a corn husk is tasty and portable, but it is labor-intensive and sometimes messy. The Chicago tamale takes this basic idea, but instead of chunk meat and masa, it uses ground meat and spices covered with a layer of cornmeal mush, pressed, and rolled into cylinders like large, fat cigars. Wrapped in paper or, later, cellophane, it became the perfect portable snack.

This recipe contains elements of what the Pennsylvania Dutch call "scrapple," which is leftover meat cooked with corn meal. Also added are spices like garlic, chili powder, and salt. Selling them on the street is a custom borrowed from not only Central America but African American migrants from the deep South who created a dish inspired by Mexican immigrants who often worked beside them. This custom was documented in early blues songs such as Herbert Ingraham's "Hot Tamale Man" (1909) and the greatest of all pre-war bluesmen Robert Johnson. In his song, "They Are Red Hot," he sang, "Hot tamales they are red hot yes, she's got them for sale."

During the Great Depression, Chicago's streets were filled with pushcarts selling everything from hot dogs (which eventually became the Chicago hot dog) to ice cream. The idea came about to sort of turn the tamale into a hot dog, something that can be eaten by hand on the go. Thus, the

Chicago tamale, an amalgamation of peoples' ideas, was born. This included two Greek men, both named Athanasius. They became partners, buying a bakery that was opened in 1937 that produced hot dog buns. Adding the Chicago snack was another source of income, and Tom Tom Tamales, Chicago's oldest and one of many Chicago tamale manufacturers on the near south side, was born. Although they are sold throughout the Chicago area, the Chicago Tamale seems to be particularly prevalent on Chicago's near south side in the neighborhoods around the Chicago White Sox ballpark, Guaranteed Rate Field. In these neighborhoods, you can see other ways tamales are served. These include the "Mother-in-Law," which is two tamales on a hot dog bun smothered with chili. Some say that the name comes from the fact that it was invented by somebody's mother-in-law, but locals, like the late Johnny Veliotis, claim that it was given the moniker because "like your mother-in-law it causes heartburn." This sandwich was sampled by none other than Anthony Bourdain, who described the dish that he sampled at Fat Johnnies at 7242 S. Western Ave. as being "disturbing in design yet strangely compelling."

Malört

On June 21, 2019, Mick Jagger stood onstage at Soldier Field and exclaimed to an audience of 70,000 people, including myself, "We have played Chicago 38 or 39 times, and I still haven't had an Italian beef or a shot of Malört." The fact that the crown prince of rock and roll identified both products is an indication of their worldwide fame. Strong, tough, of ethnic origins, Malört fits Chicago's working-class image perfectly. Established in 1934, Malört is derived from beskbrannvinn, a Swedish liquor with supposed medicinal properties, made with wormwood. Swedish immigrant Carl Jeppson arrived in the United States in the late 1880s and settled on N. Clark St. in what was then a burgeoning Swedish community. With memories of "bask," Jeppson decided to make his own version in small batches, probably in a back room or garage. Jeppson sold his product out of a suitcase, door to door. During Prohibition he claimed it was cough medicine. Local legend has it that Chicago police officers stopped Jeppson while peddling Malört, took one sip, and said something to the effect of "anything that tastes this bad has to be medicine."

The Malört website states that a company named Bielzoff Products bought the recipe for Malört at the end of Prohibition. The company's vice-president, a man named George Brode, bought out the company in the early 1940s. Brode was a 1933 graduate of Northwestern

University Law School. Throughout his life he manufactured and sold liquor as a hobby. Malört continued to be somewhat of a "mom-and-pop," small-batch operation. After hiring Patricia Gabelick as his secretary in 1966, Brode began ceding more and more of the business of Malört to her, concentrating on his law practice. But like the alcohol itself, Malört's popularity continued to ferment. Hard living tradesmen began adopting the drink as their own. Soon, the students and young Millennials known as "hipsters" began to find Malört. With the advent of social media, young people started posting pictures and later videos of unsuspecting drinkers convulsing in what is now known widely as "a Malört face."

A young man named Tremaine Atkinson began to work part-time at Malört, helping Gabelick with marketing. Due to Malört's rising popularity and the tripling of sales, the company was actually having trouble finding enough wormwood for production, a problem that Atkinson helped to solve. After several attempts over the next five years, Gabelick finally relented and sold the recipe, rights, and enterprise of Malört to Atkinson. Malört is now part of CH Distilleries, located on S. Clinton St.

Fighting Gangster Stereotypes

Today, Chicago's Italian American population is known primarily for their introduction of Italian beef, deep-dish pizza, and unfortunately, gangsters from the Prohibition era. Yet Italians have played an important role in the city since the days before it was even a city. The first Italian to come to what would become Chicago arrived in the Fall of 1680. Enrico Tonti passed through the Chicago portage, making him the first Italian to venture into Chicagoland. While small numbers trickled in over the following decades, the major wave of Italians arrived in the city at the end of the 19th century. Fleeing from poverty, the Italians who arrived in Chicago were mainly from the southern regions, including Bari, Calabria, Messina, Naples, and some from Palermo in Sicily. They settled in the area on S. Halsted St., near Taylor St., which is still known as "Little Italy." Other Italian enclaves included the Grand and Ogden neighborhood, "The Patch" on Chicago's near north side, and the neighborhood known as "The Heart of Italy," at 24th and Oakley, which was populated by immigrants from Tuscany.

Chicago's Italian population has added much to the city's culture. Many examples of these contributions are contained within the Casa Italia. Inside the Casa's main building, the Florence Bartolomei Roselli Library is filled with books, magazines, and pamphlets detailing the lives of members of Chicago's Italian American community as well as the rich history of Italy itself. Many volumes are out of print or written by local authors and are only available at the Casa. There is also the Italians in Chicago exhibit, which includes clothing, artifacts, artwork, and photos of events such as weddings, family gatherings, and businesses that paint a picture of the lives of these immigrants and their descendants. The larger dormitory building houses the Italian American Veteran's Museum, which includes uniforms, medals, photos, and armaments that tell the story of the role Italian Americans played in fighting the numerous wars of the 20th century. The same building also houses the offices of *Fra Noi*, the Midwest's premier magazine of Italian American culture.

The Casa also hosts regular showings of Italian language films, author presentations, live music, and discussions and research on Italian culture and "finding your Italian roots." But the best part of the Casa may be its staging of grand festivals. The grounds host many Italian Saint's Day feasts (or festas), wine festivals, dances, holiday gatherings, and the annual Columbus Day feast, where as many as 2,000 revelers eat, drink, and dance at the community's largest ethnic celebration.

The Italian Cultural Center in Stone Park, Illinois

La Villita

In towns throughout Mexico, adobe arches span streets and town squares, telling everyone: You are now entering our town. In Chicago, the arch on 26th St. and Albany Ave. tells Chicagoans that they are now in Little Village, the center of Chicago's Mexican American community. Although now the most populous immigrant group in the city, Mexican Americans in Chicago were relative newcomers in the late 20th century. The group originally settled in the Pilsen neighborhood, once the stronghold of Czech and Slovak immigrants, then moved west to what was then called South Lawndale. In order to make it their

La Villita welcomes everyone.

own, in 1990, Mexican American Vietnam War veterans Ronald J. Baltierra and David Ramirez, along with then-Alderman Jesus "Chuy" Garcia, decided the neighborhood needed an identity of its own. The arch was designed by Mexican architect Adrian Lozano. The arch is made of pink adobe, and it is adorned by a sign that reads "Bienvenidos A Little Village," or Welcome to Little Village. The clock was donated by the Mexican government to Chicago's Mexican community in 1991. It was dedicated by former Mexican President Carlos Salinas de Gortari during a visit to Chicago. In January of 2022, the Chicago City Council voted unanimously to make the arch an official Chicago Landmark.

Italian Beef

Paper-thin sliced roast beef and green peppers soaking in a beef gravy flavored with garlic, oregano, and other seasonings. Place it on fresh, crispy French or Italian bread and top it off with a blend known as giardiniera, and you have the Italian beef sandwich. The recent airing of *The Bear*, a Hulu/FX series about a topflight chef who returns to his hometown to run an Italian beef stand, has brought the sandwich national attention. But

Chicagoans have known about it for almost 100 years, ever since the sandwich was invented by the immigrants living in Little Italy on W. Taylor St.. For them, red meat was a luxury served only at weddings and other special occasions. Celebrants

found a way to stretch it by slicing it super thin, covering it with inexpensive green peppers, flavoring it with gravy, and stuffing it in a roll. Thus was born the Italian beef sandwich.

Al Ferrari, his sister Frances, and her husband, Chris Pacelli, got the idea that this sandwich could also be served during the week to workers and neighborhood folks. In 1938, they opened a sidewalk stand at Harrison and Laflin Sts. before moving to the present location on nearby Taylor St. Over the years many other Italian beef stands opened, and dozens of hot dog and hamburger shacks throughout the city have made the sandwich a featured item. But with *The Bear*, the sandwich has now hit the national spotlight.

San Juan in Chicago

When you drive down Division St. near Damen on Chicago's north side, the businesses, signs, and artwork make you feel like you are almost in Puerto Rico. But if that is not enough to let you know, the stretch between Damen and California is marked by two 60-foot-high Puerto Rican flags that stretch across Division St. Many businesses and façades are also named, or look, as if they are in old San Juan, with cast-iron decorations and artwork.

Puerto Ricans began to settle in the former German enclave of Humboldt Park during the late 1960s. The gentrification of Lincoln Park, and later Wicker Park, in the 1980s and 1990s forced many more Chicagoans of Puerto Rican descent to move into the area. Soon the neighborhood was home to an estimated 60,000 Puerto Ricans. As you walked down the street on a summer's day, musicians could be heard playing bongos and cuatros in backyards and on street corners. The sounds of salsa, merengue, and later reggaeton blared first from hi-fi stereos, then portable "boom boxes," and now music downloaded from cell phones. Puerto Rican events like Three Kings Day, the Haunted Paseo Boricua, and especially the annual parade and festival celebrating Puerto Rican Culture (Puerto Rican Day) that takes place on the second weekend of June, fill the neighborhood and bring visitors from throughout the Midwest. Roberto Clemente High School, named after the Hall of Fame ballplayer of Puerto Rican heritage, was built in the 1970s.

In addition to artwork and music, the Paseo also features plenty of Puerto Rican culinary specialties. These include traditional favorites like "arroz y gandules," which is made from yellow rice, small pigeon peas (gandules), olive oil, spices, and sometimes ham or sausage. Another Puerto Rican delicacy is Lechon, a slow-cooked pork that is roasted for up to 12 hours, it combines the best of roasting and barbecue. Humboldt Park also has its own original contribution to Puerto Rican cuisine, the jibarito. Introduced by restauranteur Peter Figueroa in 1996, it is a basic Puerto Rican or Cuban sandwich featuring steak or pork with lettuce, cheese, and a spicy aioli with a twist. Instead of using bread, the fillings are placed between two pieces of fried plantain for a unique, crispy crust. The sandwiches are available throughout Humboldt Park along Division, North Ave. and Fullerton, other neighborhood shops, and even in Puerto Rico!

This unique sculpture is a symbol for Chicago's Puerto Rican community.

Keeping the Blues Alive

Blues music came from the deep south via Africa, but it found a home in Chicago. It is here that artists like Muddy Waters and Howlin' Wolf gained international fame. But while artists like Waters and Buddy Guy eventually played in stadiums, Chicago blues began in small, neighborhood clubs. Some of the more heralded venues included Theresa's, Silvios, Pepper's Lounge, the Chicken Shack, and the Zanzibar. It was here that the first waves of the Great Migration supported their homegrown culture. Unlike more upscale night clubs, the blues lounges were usually neighborhood bars where the beer was cheap.

During the late 1960s and '70s, the blues and their followers moved north to Chicago's Old Town and Lincoln Park neighborhoods. Here a new generation of blues fans, mostly white "hippies," discovered the music via groups like The Rolling Stones. With its location in the working class, racially mixed

Still Home of the Blues

Chicago has many other venues that celebrate its great blues legacy. The best-known is Buddy Guy's Blues Legends. Opened and owned by the man who most agree is the greatest living blues artist, Legends is located at 700 S. Wabash Ave. Guy's presence has attracted stars like Eric Clapton, Stevie Ray Vaughan, David Bowie, The Rolling Stones, ZZ Top, and many others to visit and make impromptu appearances. It also has magnificent southern-style food and a blues museum filled with Guy's artifacts and awards. Kingston Mines at 2558 N. Halsted St. is the last of the old Lincoln Park blues clubs, while Blue Chicago, at 536 N. Clark St., is the premier blues club on Chicago's near north side.

Humboldt Park neighborhood, Rosa's Lounge returned to the south and west side, neighborhood blues club tradition. The club was opened in 1984 by Tony Mangiullo, an immigrant from Italy, and his mother, Rosa, at 3420 W. Armitage Ave. in Chicago's Humboldt Park neighborhood. Tony and Rosa had a much more personal, "down home" approach to the blues. "Mama Rosa" would often make home-cooked, Italian meals for guests and performers. There was also a small apartment upstairs where visiting performers and musicians sometimes stayed. This simple, informal vibe attracted many of the old-time greats from the rural south like Homesick James, Pinetop Perkins, Junior Wells, and Honeyboy Edwards. Younger performers like Sugar Blue, made famous for his work on The Rolling Stones's "Miss You," were also attracted to this more traditional approach. Other up-and-coming artists of the time like Billy Branch and Melvin Taylor found that Rosas was a place where they could expand their musical horizons. Today Rosas continues this Chicago tradition with blues seven nights a week.

Chicago's Hillbilly Home

Just like the Great Migration brought African Americans from states like Mississippi, Louisiana, and Alabama to many of Chicago's south side neighborhoods, during the 1950s and '60s whites from the mountain regions of Kentucky and Tennessee traveled northward to find jobs in factories and construction. During the 1960s and '70s, if you took a walk down Clark St. or Broadway near Wilson you would be sure to see hosts of men sporting Elvis-like sideburns and hair slicked back with the help of generous dabs of Vitalis. These southern transplants transformed Chicago's Uptown neighborhood into what became known as "Hillbilly Heaven."

Many of these migrants have moved back home, but many others simply lost their accents and blended in with the general population. There are still some remnants of this culture in "ham off the bone" diners, but if there is one repository of the country culture in Chicago it is Carol's Pub. The bar was opened by Ted Harris in 1972, when the hillbilly presence was still strong in Uptown. At that time, men with greased-back hair and women in simple white dresses could be seen walking around the areas of Clark, Wilson, Lawrence, and Broadway.

"When we came here in 1972, Uptown was booming," says Carol Harris, namesake and former owner of Carol's. "Most of the people here were Appalachians, and my husband Ted was from Alabama. He knew country people and country music and saw opening a country bar as a great business opportunity."

With a 4:00 a.m. closing license, Carol's was known as a late-night place where you could hear country music, drink cheap beer, and maybe watch the occasional bar fight. As the '80s turned into the '90s many of the original southern migrants went home or died off, but the bar's gritty scenery, live music, and cheap beer drew many younger "new-wave" customers. Carol's is known for live music, and its house band, Diamondback, played there for almost 30 years.

The stage and sound system were good. I personally played there as part of many bands and jam sessions from 2012 until the bar closed in September of 2016. Hanging wires, drywall that hadn't been painted, and aging ownership signaled that the end was near. But after a two-year hiatus, the bar reopened in December of 2018. In October of 2022, the band Wilco performed a surprise set at the small bar, much to the amazement of many lucky fans. Today is still boasts live country music every weekend, as bands with names like The Trailer Park Twisters, and Dalton and the Sheriffs are keeping the tradition alive.

The former Rapp Mansion, site of the "Beer Baron Murder," is just one of the many reminders of Chicago's crime-ridden past and the hauntings which were often the result. Photo by Jennifer Ann Stix

Chapter 6

Dark Tales: A City Rich in Crime and Its Haunting Legacy

From its first white settler—who was a murderer and land cheat—Chicago has always had a violent, corrupt, and grim history. During the 19th and early 20th centuries, its citizens worked long hours in dangerous factories or at places like the Union Stockyards, where they were continuously surrounded by blood and the stench of death. Immigrants, the poor, and others have been exploited and even murdered as part of a long-standing tradition of crooked politicians, gangsters, and thieves. Even today, when one applies for a city job, they are first asked, "Who's your Chinaman?" a racist phrase that essentially means "which crooked politician did you pay off to get this job?" So, it is no wonder that Chicago's history or corruption and crime has left not only a legacy of gangsters, criminals, and killers, but also a haunted history, where the cries of victims can still be heard in ghostly sights throughout the city.

The Beer Baron Murder

There is a line of French Second Empire, Queen Anne, and Gothic limestone mansions that occupy Hoyne Ave. between North Ave. and Evergreen St. in Chicago's Wicker Park neighborhood. Called Beer Baron Row, it was occupied by German immigrants who brought the skills of brewing with them from their native land. One of the most prosperous of these was John Raap, who made a fortune selling beer and wine and was later murdered by his own employee over part of that fortune.

In a time before refrigeration, soft drinks, and juices, these men made vast fortunes selling beer to a thirsty immigrant population. But despite their wealth, they were immigrants, so they were not accepted by the landed gentry like Marshall Field, Montgomery Ward, and Potter Palmer, who settled in the Prairie Ave. and Gold Coast regions. They also wanted to be near their "market" of German and Scandinavian immigrants, so these newly minted millionaires settled just west of Milwaukee Ave.

John Raap was a German immigrant who owned feed stores and served in the Union Army during the Civil War before going into the domestic liquor business. His growing success allowed him to build what is still considered to be the most spectacular mansion on the row. Sitting on over a quarter acre of land, it boasts Victorian, English, and kitchen gardens that surround the home on three sides. The building itself is a four-story structure comprised of red brick and containing 22 rooms inside of 8,200 square feet of space. Besides its fourth-floor dormer windows jutting out of its Mansard roof, it has a large copper turret that overlooks the entire neighborhood.

But in many cases, money brings problems. Such was the case between Rapp and his employee G. H. Braunschweig.

Braunschweig was caught embezzling $2,300 (about $80,000 today) and brought before a grand jury in 1897. In order to avoid embarrassment, Braunschweig proposed giving Raap two lots worth $1,000 each in exchange for the money he had taken from his employer. Raap would not compromise and demanded cash or Braunschweig's home. As the sheriff was about to arrest Braunschweig, the accused asked if he could try one more time to settle the matter with Raap. The sheriff reluctantly agreed, and Braunschweig was brought to Raap's place of business. After being released from his handcuffs, Braunschweig approached his accuser. But instead of talking, Braunschweig produced a revolver and shot Raap in the head and then turned the gun on himself.

Some say due to the murder that the Raap mansion is haunted, but the newest owners did not seem to care, as in 2021 they paid an estimated $4.8 million dollars, for the property.

This Wicker Park Mansion was the site of the "Beer Baron Murder."
Photo by Jennifer Ann Stix

Haunted Death Alley

On the afternoon of December 31, 1903, over 600 people were burned alive in what is still the deadliest fire in American history. It started out as a festive holiday event. The play, a children's comedy called *Mr. Bluebeard*, was being performed in front of a packed house, mostly of mothers who had taken their children to see the sights and lights of downtown and a play at the brand-new Iroquois Theater, which had opened early to accommodate the holiday season. The first act went fine, but into the second act a spotlight burst. Flames began to appear backstage. The area was filled with cloth costumes, wooden props, and canvas backdrops soaked in oil. The fire began to rage. The asbestos curtain, intended to act as a fire stop, did not come down. The seats, cloth, straw, and wooden stage ignited. The cast opened a back door, which tragically created a backdraft effect and flames raged across the ceiling as if somebody had lit a gas grill. As people ran for the exits, they found more tragedy. Many of the exit doors and windows had been shuttered with plywood or deadbolts to keep unpaid customers from entering. The exits were not lit. Even worse, the exit doors opened inward, so as the crowd rushed them, they pressed against the doorways, sealing their fate.

Some of the patrons in the balcony and upper floors were able to escape by crawling across wooden planks that were set in front of the windows. But the planks were unsteady and the going was slow, so mothers—often holding their children's hands—tried to jump, meeting a cruel death in the alley below. This may be the reason for the sounds of eerie screams and the sights of turn-of-the-century mothers with their children wandering in the alley that have been reported for decades.

Almost ghoulishly, the theater was quickly reopened. In 1926, the Oriental Theater was built on the same spot. It later reopened as the Ford Theater, where, ironically, its first performance was *Ragtime.* Through the years, actors have reported feeling cold spots and hearing noises, especially in the dressing room. The most recent may be Anna Gasteyer. The *Saturday Night Live* alum told CBS 2 Chicago that while rehearsing *Wicked* she would hear children's voices. Other performers stated that they would see apparitions of families, dressed in period clothing, suddenly appear and disappear. Sometimes it was just children, hands out, crying, looking for a mother who was no

Ghosts are said to haunt "Death Alley."

longer there. On certain dark, rainy nights, as well as on warm summer evenings, these figures continue to roam and haunt the area, their souls still not at peace after their fiery deaths.

Chicago's Haunted River

In a city filled with grim days filled with murder, and death, this may have been the worst. On July 24, 1915, the *Eastland*, a giant luxury passenger ship, capsized in the Chicago River, killing more people than the *Titanic*. Even before the boat hit the water, many were mangled by falling debris and sliding furniture. Others were crushed by the mass of human bodies as the ship turned over. Most drowned, unable to move or swim away as they were trapped beneath the boat. Finally, many, having made it to air pockets within the ship, suffocated while listening to firemen and welders who desperately tried to rescue them by cutting the steel bottom of the boat from above.

It began as a warm July day. Employees from the Western Electric Company began boarding the ship for a day-long excursion to the beaches and fresh air near Michigan City, Indiana. These passengers were mostly immigrants from eastern and southern Europe. They worked 10-hour days and came home to cramped apartments with no yards or porches, often with shared bathrooms. So many wanted to escape their dreary lives that the ship quickly became loaded far beyond its capacity. Yet the greedy ship owners ignored this, taking every ticket fee they could get. Even before the ship left the dock it had begun to tilt slightly, and the crew took more water into the ballasts. At 7:15 a.m. the boat left port, but it continued to list. At 7:28 a.m. it tilted to a 45-degree angle. Pianos and furniture slid, people began to panic, and soon the boat completely capsized. Unlike the *Titanic*, there was no time even to attempt to pass out life jackets or launch lifeboats. While the river water was warm, we must remember in those days women wore long dresses and

men suits, which weighed them down like anchors. Those who could swim were trapped as the channel was so narrow there was no room to surface. The efforts of firemen, sailors, and passersby to rescue the passengers were heroic. Many were saved, and the injured were so numerous that Marshall Fields was converted into a temporary hospital. But 844 were not. They lay in makeshift morgues in warehouses along the river.

There have been many rumors of the area being haunted. For decades, boaters claimed that at night they heard moaning and screaming for help. Sometimes they saw bodies in long, white gowns floating in the water, or outstretched arms reaching up from the murky depths. There are also reports of cold breezes appearing in midsummer, only to disappear into the wind.

The Frank Nitti Museum and Former Home

Frank Nitti is Chicago's second most famous, or infamous, gangster. Beginning his career as the bodyguard for Al Capone, Nitti became the head of Capone's underworld empire after "Scarface" was sent to prison in 1931. Although known as "The Enforcer," Nitti was more of an executive than violent criminal. Nonetheless, he was portrayed as a machine-gun-toting tough guy in the long-running TV series *The Untouchables*, as well as in the 1987 feature film of the same name. In later films, including *The Road to Perdition* and *Public Enemies*, Nitti was also depicted on the big screen, but more as the man giving orders for assassinations or the extortion of Hollywood movie studios.

Frank Nitti's safe

In 1942, Nitti married his third wife, Annette Caravetta-Nitti, who was the secretary for one of Al Capone's lawyers. The Nitti's had a large apartment on the fourth floor of the Varnish Building that became their Chicago residence and headquarters. Nitti committed suicide while walking along the railroad tracks of his Riverside "country" home in 1943. But that did not stop Caravetta, who went on to become one of America's most powerful female mobsters.

It is alleged Caravetta had mob accountant Alex Greenberg killed over two million dollars. With that money, Caravetta bought the entire Varnish Building. Here, she ran her own mob operation under the guise of the Caravetta Food Company, which sold olive oil and Parmesan cheese out of a first-floor storefront. Using as many as seven different aliases, Caravetta continued to run her crime empire from the Varnish Building until her death.

After it became Harry Caray's restaurant, an electrician accidentally drilled through a wall and discovered an 85-foot-long room with 16-foot ceilings in the basement. Connected to underground tunnels running from the street, it was Nitti's headquarters. According to the video, *Frank Nitti's Vault*, produced by the restaurant, Nitti also has a secret vault, which still rests undisturbed behind a wall. While the vault remains closed to the public, the basement of Harry Caray's Italian Steakhouse has been converted into a de facto Frank Nitti Museum. Lining the staircase walls are original photos, newspaper clippings, and other exhibits depicting the lives and careers of Nitti and Caravetta. Among other sights are the many subpoenas served to Nitti throughout his criminal career, a phonebook with the names and phone numbers of some of Chicago's most famous crime figures, and a safe that allegedly held Nitti's treasured belongings.

Harry Caray and a Gangster Museum

Today, the museum and vault are part of Harry Caray's Italian Steakhouse, started by the famed baseball announcer. Along with the Nitti museum, the restaurant boasts a small sports museum dedicated to Caray. Both can be visited free of charge to customers and curious tourists, and there are even "gangster tours."

The "Crime of the Century"

This Chicago crime captivated the entire nation. Richard Loeb and Nathan Leopold, two highly educated young men from wealthy families, thought themselves somehow superior and not governed by normal laws or morality. In order to prove it to each other and the world, they plotted to commit a murder, and they were convinced their superior intelligence would allow them to get away with it. For weeks they plotted the murder, eventually picking 14-year-old Robert "Bobby" Franks as their victim. Like the two men, Franks was from a wealthy family of the Jewish faith. Even more disturbing, Franks was Loeb's second cousin and lived across the street. They coerced Franks into a borrowed car, where he was bludgeoned to death with a chisel. The duo then drove to Wolf Lake, an industrial area just outside of Chicago, where his body was doused in acid and left in a ditch. The young men were apparently not as smart as they thought. Several clues, including Franks's eyeglasses, a typewriter on which a ransom note was printed, and the testimony of Leopold's chauffer, landed the two young men in jail for murder. The proceeding trail and murder were soon labeled, "the crime of the century." Through testimony, it was disclosed that Leopold and Loeb were in a homosexual relationship and that the murder was also an act to prove their mutual love. The defendants' family wealth allowed them to hire famed attorney Clarence Darrow, whose impassioned speech kept both men from receiving the death penalty. Loeb died in Statesville Prison, the victim of over 50 stab wounds from a man who claimed Loeb made homosexual advances towards him. Leopold served his time in prison, eventually married, and spent the remainder of his life in Puerto Rico, where he published a book about the native birds. Franks will forever be remembered as the most innocent of victims. His childhood home and the site of his funeral were located in what is still known as "The Franks Mansion." For many years it served as a kindergarten and preschool, but it has recently been bought and renovated by private interests.

Little has changed since 1924 at the former Franks Mansion.

Resurrection Mary, Chicago's Greatest Ghost

A young woman dressed in white is walking on Archer Ave. along the lonely, wooded stretch near the former Oh Henry and later Willowbrook Ballroom. Under the beam of headlights from an approaching car, the figure would suddenly appear, arm outstretched. Between the darkness and the flowing white dress, she was hard to make out, except for the fact that she was young and beautiful.

"Do you need a ride somewhere?" a driver would ask.

Without a sound or answer the woman would get into the car, but when the car would drive by the Resurrection Cemetery, the woman would vanish.

There have been several reports and eyewitness accounts of the figure. The first was from a man named Jerry Paulus, who, in 1936, spent the night dancing with a stunning young woman, dressed in white, at the Oh Henry Ballroom. He volunteered to drive her home, but as the car passed the graveyard, he stated that the figure floated out of the car towards the graveyard. These stories continued into the 1980s, when witnesses say a woman with curly blonde hair and wearing what looked like an old wedding dress was seen near another dance club called Harlow's at 8058 S. Cicero Ave. The figure also has been said to have ordered a drink and then promptly disappeared at Chet's Melody Lounge, which is directly across the street from the cemetery.

Although there are many versions of the story behind this ghost, they all begin with a woman sneaking out of her home to go dancing. After a time, she settles on one young man as a dance partner. As the clock strikes 1:30 a.m. he offers her a ride home. Some accounts say he tries to kiss her during the ride. After telling him to stop, Mary realizes her only option is escape. In a panic, she opens the doors of the moving car and jumps out, but an oncoming car fails to see her and takes Mary's life. Some say the woman in the story was a Polish girl named Mary Bregovy. Others say it was a woman named Ana Norkus. But everyone agrees that during the 1980s the iron bars on the fence at Resurrection Cemetery were pried apart, and the small handprints of a young woman were burnt into the iron. Time after time cemetery workers would try to restore the bars, but they would not take paint. Apparently, officials from the Archdiocese of Chicago were called to no avail. In 2019, the section of fence was replaced. Over the years, the sightings of Mary have become less frequent. But every day the bartender at Chet's Melody Lounge places a Bloody Mary on the bar, hoping that Mary will return to finish it.

The Haunted Circus Train Wreck

Hammond, Indiana, railyard, June 22, 1918, 4:00 a.m. Alonzo Sargent, train engineer, was moving 20 empty Pullman cars to another spot in the yard. Just ahead of him, an estimated 400 trapeze artists, strongmen, lion tamers, clowns, roustabouts, barkers, and staff from the Hagenbeck-Wallace Circus occupied the train on the tracks ahead. After traveling all night, they were trying to get a little more sleep before setting up for their next show. Possibly tired, or weak from kidney pills, Sargent gripped the throttle and moved forward. As the train eased ahead, the motion, pills, and lack of sleep in the dim morning light led Sargent to close his eyes. He began getting sleepy. He closed his eyes again. This time, he did not reopen them. But he did not lose his grip on the throttle. His car blew past two stop signals and continued to gain speed. The train slammed into the circus cars. Lit by oil lamps and filled with straw, the wooden circus cars flared up almost instantaneously. Half asleep and trapped inside, the victims had no chance. Emergency workers tried to put out the fire, but as the *Indianapolis Star* reported, "the rescuers were compelled to stand by helpless and hysterical as they listened to the agonized screams of human beings slowly burned to death." As dawn arrived, the wreck kept burning. Even at noon the next day it was reported that a clown named "Big Joe" Coyle was still trying to rescue his wife and children and had to be dragged away. He later said he wished he had died with them.

In the end, 86 people were reported to have died and 127 were injured. Most of the victims were burned so badly they could not be identified. Instead, they were buried in a mass grave in the Woodlawn Cemetery with funds provided by Showman's Rest, an organization dedicated to caring for retired circus performers. Since many of the victims were roustabouts, many of the graves are simply designated by "Unknown Male," and "Unknown Female." The area is marked by several white granite elephants. Despite popular myth, the car containing the circus animals arrived separately, and none were killed in the fire. But it is said that on some nights, after all the visitors have left, people can hear the cries of the circus elephants, mourning for their dead masters. And some claim that if you listen hard enough, you can hear the playing of the organ and the clapping of the audience and see the spotlights of the circus flashing against the night sky.

A granite elephant marks the haunted spot at the Showmen's Rest Cemetery.

Voodoo and Hoodoo in Chicago

The following was taken from the 1946 catalog for the King Novelty Company, located at 2234 S. Cottage Grove Ave.:

"Big Hand Curio Outfit—The Outfit contains a Big Mojo Hand Curio Bag, filled with Lodestone, High John the Conqueror Root, Hand Root, and the Devil's Shoestring."

Besides blues music, soul food, and countless other contributions, the Great Migration brought another aspect of southern black culture to Chicago: voodoo, and its more urban, commercial offspring hoodoo. Many are familiar with voodoo—a set of spiritual practices brought to the New World by African slaves and forced underground by the white power structure in the south—from stories from New Orleans. Hoodoo was born out of the suppression of the original voodoo practices. Smaller and more personal, it involved (among other things) the use of roots, charms, and spiritual goods. For many African Americans who migrated to Chicago, this was part of the culture and their daily lives, and was referred to in the work of blues artists like Junior Wells ("Hoodoo Man Blues"), Lonnie Brooks ("Two Headed Man"), and Muddy Waters ("Got My Mojo Workin'").

One of the longest-running spiritual supply stores was the L. W. De Laurence Company, located for many years in an office building at 180 N. Wabash Ave. According to the book, *Spiritual Merchants*, the company was owned by a man named Morton

Newman. The largest such company in the nation, Valamor, also ran King Novelty Company. King's catalogs, known for their colorful artwork featuring black cats, scantily clad females in turbans, and exaggerated claims, were distributed throughout the country. The south side was also home to many neighborhood "root doctors," who worked out of their homes selling these products along with personal advice.

For many years, Augustine's Spiritual Goods, run by Frank "Papa Doc" Steele Pulaski at 3114 S. Halsted St., kept this tradition alive, but as the first-generation migrants began to die off, much of the traditional African American hoodoo in Chicago did as well.

Voodoo in Chicago Today

Today, this practice of Hoodoo has become amalgamated with new age, metaphysical, and occult beliefs, but supplies are still available at:

- **The Lucah Spiritual Voodoo Store**, at 1024 N. Kedvale Ave. The store sells lodestones, candles, herbs, roots, and amulets and prepares personal magic bags.
- **Augustine's Spiritual Boutique**, 3327 S. Halsted St. Purchased from Pulaski, the store sells candles, incense, sprays and body washes, quartz and other chakra crystals, oils, herbs, and roots, including John the Conqueror Root.
- **Maliway Brothers Spells, Charms and Potions**, 1407 W. Morse Ave. This north side store deals with more Anglo-Saxon based "magic," including Wicca, and the owners even take groups on special "field trips" to outdoor locations to connect with pagan spirits.

Museum of Circus Freaks and Murderers

When you first walk into Graveface Records, it looks like a "normal" alternative record store with an array of vinyl records, along with horror and music DVDs. Yet the back of the store takes you into a sordid world of natural and manmade exhibits that will shock even the bravest of souls. Among the exhibits are a two headed calf, a cyclops cow, human skeletons, shrunken heads, and a recreation of John Wayne Gacy's jail cell containing much of his original artwork. There is also a vast exhibit on America's not-so-proud tradition of carnival "freaks," featuring photos and exhibits of "Madam Zola the Bearded Lady," 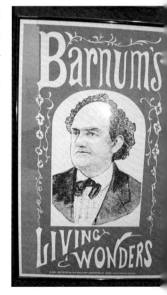 "Alligator Boy," "the Siamese Twins," "The Ossified Man," and many more. These types of museums/exhibits were popular across America during the middle and late 19th century. Before he started his circus, P. T. Barnum made his fortune operating his American Museum, which opened in 1842. It advertised that it contained, "a million wonders," including animal specimens from around the world, shrunken heads, and live exhibits and performances by oddities such as "Tom Thumb."

"I collect what are known as 'gaffes' in the tradition of the old dime museums or Ripley's Believe It or Not Museum," Ryan Graveface, the owner and curator says. "Except where much of the material in those places was fake, mine is real."

Graveface has been collecting oddities and the belongings of famous criminals and mass murderers for over 40 years. Most are displayed in a much larger museum of the same type in Savannah, Georgia, which contains two stories and 5,600 square feet of exhibits. "Believe it or not," he was running out of room and needed to expand.

"I used to live in Chicago and miss it," Graveface says. "I always wanted to open a store that sold not only records and horror DVDs, but also wanted to have a museum dedicated to circus sideshows, true crime, oddities, and UFOs."

Graveface has accumulated many of the letters, drawings, and personal effects of John Wayne Gacy, and other serial killers like Ed Gein, who many see as the inspiration for Hannibal Lecter, and Aileen Carol Wournos, the Florida sex worker and mass murderer portrayed in the movie *Monster*. As of now Graveface Records is a small shop in Chicago's "hip" Wicker Park neighborhood, but Graveface will be expanding soon.

"I have big plans for not only the store but a much larger museum," Graveface says. "We are looking for locations now."

In the meantime, if you want your fix of horror not on a screen, then Graveface Records is the place to go.

A two headed calf is just one of the many oddities on display at the Graveface Museum.

Jeffrey Dahmer's Stalking Grounds

Chicago has many infamous and unfortunate connections to gangsters, violent criminals, and mass murderers, from Al Capone to Richard Speck, John Gacy, and many more. It would seem that the Windy City would have been spared the horrors of Jeffery Dahmer, as he lived in and committed most of his crimes in Milwaukee. But alas, Chicago does not get off so easily. It seems that this horrific serial killer, whose life was chronicled in a highly rated Netflix series, came to Chicago to look for victims. Although there were many places the serial killer stalked potential victims, the one most mentioned and chronicled was the L&L Tap. The bar is located at Belmont and Clark, four blocks south of Wrigley Field. Today the neighborhood is filled with shiny

Jeffrey Dahmer stalked young victims at the L&L Tap, once called "the creepiest bar in the US."

new high-rises, bars, and businesses. But in the 1980s, the area was much different. With stores like The Alley, the intersection of Clark and Belmont was the headquarters for Chicago's leather, tattoo, and punk rock scene. In particular, a Dunkin' Donuts store was located where a Target store stands today. Known as "Punkin' Donuts," it became a major source of drugs, alcohol, and prostitution, largely among older teens and young adults. Dahmer would sit at a window table at the L&L, peering across the street in search of victims. In fact, several sources state that when an L&L employee named Frankie saw Dahmer being arrested on television he screamed, "Oh my God, that's the guy that used to sit in the window and stare at the kids."

Although it was once named "the creepiest bar in the US," the L&L was also voted "Chicago's Best Dive Bar," was featured in Anthony Bourdain's Travel Channel Series, *The Layover*, and was a location for the HBO series *Lovecraft Country*. It is also one of the few places left in the neighborhood where an old guy on a pension can get a beer for under five dollars.

The "Richard Speck Hotel"

Today it is a beautiful stone building, a remnant of Chicago's great era of architecture, in the heart of River North. Surrounded by shiny high-rises, law offices, and boutique restaurants, the building's beauty hides its connection to what was then the most hideous mass murder in Chicago's history. On July 14, 1966, Richard Speck strangled and stabbed eight student nurses on Chicago's southeast side.

At the time, Speck was working as a member of the Merchant Marine, whose Union Hall was at 2335 100th St. During the preceding months, Speck's lifelong criminal history, which began with arrests for petty burglary and assault as a teen, had slowly escalated to alleged assault, armed assault, rape, and even murder. He had served minor stints in prison, but for the major offenses (such as the death of barmaid Mary Pierce), he had been questioned and released. In 1966, Speck found work with the Merchant Marine, but in June

Mass murderer Richard Speck once lived at 648 N Dearborn St.

and July he was promised a job on a merchant vessel, only to be replaced on the ship by a seaman with more seniority. As his failures mounted, so did his anger. At 11:00 p.m. on July 13th he broke into a townhouse, possibly to conduct a burglary. What he found inside was a dormitory for student nurses. He killed eight of them by brutally slashing them with a knife. He raped his final victim. One woman, Corazon Amurao, a Filipino exchange student nurse, survived by hiding under a bed. Speck left the scene and then calmly had a drink and a hamburger at a bar near the Maritime headquarters a few blocks from the murder scene early on the morning of the 14th. He then took a cab to Old Town and walked south to the Raleigh Hotel. While the news of the murders rocked the city and its media, Speck hired a prostitute, who somehow suspected he may have been the killer. According to a *Chicago Tribune* article and later book by Dennis Breo, the police came to the Raleigh Hotel, entered Room 806, and found Speck and a gun. But once again, he was let go. That evening, the hotel desk clerk, Otha Hullinger, saw Speck in the lobby and showed him the account in the newspaper. Speck angrily left, leaving with his possessions in a plastic bag. A short time later the police arrived and showed Hullinger a picture of the suspect. When she saw it, she said, "Oh my God, its him."

Speck was soon arrested and sentenced to death, but his sentence was commuted to concurrent life sentences. Today, as workers dressed in suits carrying cups of latte walk by the building, few know about its sinister past.

Old St. James and the Ghosts of Monk's Castle

Located just outside of Chicago at 1600 Archer Ave. in Lemont, Illinois, it is one of the few structures in Chicagoland that still exists from the 19th century. Because of its age, one can see why many tales of ghosts and haunting are centered around it. The original congregation began in a log cabin in 1833. There is evidence, however, that Catholic services were held here much earlier. Father Jacques Marquette and Louis Joliet arrived nearby in 1673, at was then a Potawatomi village. The explorers stopped to trade with the Indians. Later, a very ill Father Marquette wintered here, near the healing waters of Willow Springs.

A century and a half later, Irish immigrants began to settle the area southwest of Chicago and petitioned for a priest. In 1833, Father John Mary Irenaeus St. Cyr, appointed to Old St. Mary's that same year, began holding services. Many more Irish immigrants arrived to work on the nearby Illinois and Michigan Canal. The growing congregation raised

the money to build a church made from locally quarried yellow limestone. The building is now on the National Register of Historic Places.

But besides its history, the church, cemetery, and surrounding buildings are said to have been the scene of strange happenings at night. Unlike the many other Catholic churches in Chicago, it is set in an isolated stretch along Archer Ave. At night, the graveyard, church, and surrounding area are pitch black, save for the occasional flash of headlights from cars in the distance driving along Archer. This dark environment has led to many legends. Since the end of the 19th century, neighbors and passersby have reported odd sightings in the churchyard on dark nights. Shadowy figures of men in monk's robes have been seen drinking, dancing, laughing, and cavorting in the moonlight holding candles and chanting in Latin. Many say that these are the spirits of the monks, their souls finally set free, experiencing the joys of life that had eluded them in their youth. In 1977, a local police officer reported that he saw such figures one late night on patrol. He first asked, then shouted at them to stop, but there was no answer. The officer then went to his car to report the incident and retrieve a weapon. But when he emerged, the figures had all vanished.

There is another story of a finely appointed Victorian carriage traveling throughout the cemetery. A woman dressed in white emerges from the carriage, and then both the woman and carriage vanish behind the rolling hills and craggy bushes of the churchyard. It is entirely up to the reader to believe or not believe in these tales, but nevertheless, many locals still refer to it as "Monks Castle."

The Castle That Isn't Haunted

There is a giant stone castle at 632 N. Dearborn, complete with turrets and narrow windows. It has occupied this spot since 1892. Surrounded by modern glass buildings, it seems out of place. So naturally, stories of hauntings and the supernatural abound. It has been featured on the Travel Channel and Ursula Bielski's *Chicago Haunts* books. Neil Tobin, a conjurer, hosted an annual séance there on Halloween, hoping to bring back the spirit of Houdini. Yet despite its movie-location looks, much of the evidence of supernatural activity is unfounded. The Travel Channel and other outlets reported that the ghosts of victims of the Great Chicago Fire haunt the building. Yet the Chicago Fire occurred in 1871, 20 years before it was built. There were also claims about the dead bodies from the *Eastland* Disaster being stored there, their spirits roaming the

The former site of The Limelight Nightclub, said to be haunted.

structure. But all accounts indicate the bodies were stored closer to the river. Rumors of the ghost of a lawyer who committed suicide in the building have also been mentioned. But it was never a law office, and there is no record of the alleged suicide in local newspapers.

The Gallows That Stayed Open

While many believe the Excalibur Building may be haunted, there is more evidence that the old Courthouse Place/Cook County Criminal Court Building at 54 W. Hubbard St. may well be where the supernatural action is. Besides the court, part of the building contained gallows where as many as 86 men were hanged. The violent deaths of these men may have led to many unsettled spirits roaming the site, which has been refurbished and renamed as "Courthouse Place," a mixed-use development. Yet the very gallows that hung so many men had an enduring life of their own. "Terrible Tommy" O'Conner was convicted of murdering a Chicago policeman and was set to be executed in 1921, but he escaped hours before he was to face the gallows. Although hanging was later abolished as a form of punishment in Illinois, O'Conner's sentence stood, and the gallows were kept intact in the hope that he would be captured. They remained so until 1977, when a judge finally ruled that they be removed. As a macabre reminder of Chicago's past, the wooden structure was used as an exhibit in a local theme park, then purchased by Ripley's Believe or Not Museum.

Nevertheless, the building does have a great history. It has been home to the Chicago Historical Society, it was also a Moose Club, a recording studio, and several nightclubs where performers like Prince, Rihanna, and Moby took the stage. Today the building hosts Tao, an Asian-themed restaurant and nightclub.

The Grave Where Grass Doesn't Grow

In the winter of 1992, two teenage boys were showing off their coin collection to another young man, 18-year-old Stanley Brown. To them it was treasure—old silver dollars, wheat pennies, buffalo-head nickels, and so on. Yet the centerpiece was a 1957 dollar bill known as a silver certificate. Any such certificate would be rare, but this bill also had an upside-down serial number. The bill was worth a considerable amount of money, and to the teenagers it was a fortune. Brown and the boys played at each other's houses often, and one day while the two brothers were in their backyard, Brown went upstairs. Seeing the misprinted bill, Brown stuck it in his pocket.

Days went by. It was summertime and the boys played baseball almost every day in the park. One day, the brothers noticed that the silver certificate was missing. They told their father, who was furious, and instructed the boys to "beat it out of him" (Brown) the next time they played baseball.

And they did. But after the severe beating, the body lay not only bruised and bloody, but lifeless. The father and the boys took the "dead" boy to Che Che Pin Que Woods off of Irving Park Rd. just west of Cumberland. The plan was to bury the body in the woods. And they did. Brown had moved out of his parents' house, so it was a while before they filed a missing person report, and they had no idea as to his whereabouts. As months passed, the boys began to brag to their friends about "beating the boys head in out back of the shed and burying him in the woods." The rumors reached the detectives, who separated and interrogated the boys. After hours of grilling, one of the boys broke down and told them the whole story. They led the police to the spot where Brown had been buried in a shallow grave. The detectives were not sure whether he had died from the beating or suffocation, but in June of 1992, the *Chicago Tribune* reported that Clyde Rutherford and his two 16-year-old sons had been charged with the murder of Brown. Forest Preserve workers filled the exhumed grave with dirt and leveled it out. Yet as the prairie grass spread over the entire area, it would not grow on that spot. To this day, 30 years later, there is still bare earth in the section of Che Che Pin Que Woods where Stanley Brown was buried.

A boy was buried in a shallow grave in the Chicago Forest Preserve.

38,000 Lost Souls

In 1851, it was nothing but open land as far as the eyes could see. Its location was at the time the far northwest of the city limits, and the leaders of Cook County decided that it would be an ideal place to put a "poor farm" for the indigent.

Dates of the official "opening" vary but most sources say it was sometime around 1851. In 1863, the institution also began housing tuberculosis patients, and in 1870, it began admitting patients who suffered from severe mental illness. The property was then given the title of the Cook County Mental Health Center, but most people simply referred to it as "The Insane Asylum" or "Dunning" after Andrew Dunning, one of the first settlers of the area.

For a time, the site actually flourished as the residents grew vegetables and attended school. But soon it was decided that this area (located between Irving and Montrose and Narragansett and Oak Park Aves.) would also be a place where others that society did not accept—alcoholics and other mentally ill people—could be "kept away." Patients suffering from tuberculosis, destined for a long, slow death as their lungs filled with fluid until they could not breathe, were also sent there. The area between Irving Park Rd., Montrose Ave., Oak Park and Narragansett Aves. became a cruel melting pot for lost souls.

It is no wonder conditions went from bad to worse. Moaning and cries of pain and desperation filled the air at all hours. The little money for food, heating fuel, and other supplies residents had was stolen by politicians and administrators. There were reports of patients poisoning themselves or hanging themselves by bed sheets. As the years went on, things did not change. It was

Reed Mental Health Center

renamed the Reed Mental Health Center, and in 1988, the director was dismissed for what were called "deplorable conditions." These included patients being left unattended, not fed, and having what little money or possessions they may have had being taken from them. These conditions led to many patients dying from disease and neglect. Most residents had no family to care for their needs, and no funds for their burial. Upon their deaths, they were simply put in holes, sometimes called potters graves, sometimes referred to as "Boot Hill." Over the years and even decades, the bodies kept coming. With suburban sprawl, land in this area called Dunning was needed for more homes and many new ranch-style homes and apartment buildings were built throughout the 1960s, '70s and '80s. These new homeowners needed stores, schools, and recreational areas. In 1989, as the new Dunning Square Shopping Center was being built, construction workers uncovered parts of skulls, arms, and leg bones. The same was discovered as land was being excavated for the new Wilber Wright College in November of that same year. As the construction and excavation continued, the actual bodies found were in the hundreds, but estimates are that as many as 38,000 bodies had been buried there over the years. And those who now inhabit the area—customers, workers, and students from both Wilber Wright College and the nearby Taft Freshman Academy—talk of hearing moans and cries, of feeling cold breezes, and of seeing apparitions and ghostly, zombie-like figures reaching their arms through the steel gates that surround the site, beckoning children and passersby to join the rest of the bodies in the grave of lost souls.

Sources

Grossman, James R., Ann Durkin Keating and Janice L. Reiff. 2004. *The Encyclopedia of Chicago*. Chicago: University of Chicago Press.

Larson, Roy, and Mary Johnson. 2007. *Born in a Log Cabin, Alive at 175*. Chicago: The First United Methodist Church.

Kinzie, Juliette Augusta Magill. 2021. *Wau-Bun, The Early Days in the Northwest*. Originally published in 1856. Historical Society Edition. Portage, WI. Historic Preservation Society.

Wittenmeyer, Annie. *History of the Woman's Temperance Crusade: A Complete Official History*. Philadelphia, PA: Office of Christian Women.

Andreas, A. T. 1886. *History of Chicago*. Chicago, IL: A. T. Andreas.

Asbury, Herbert. 1940. *The Gangs of Chicago: An Informal History of the Chicago Underworld*. New York. Alfred Knopf.

Nolan, Mike. "Historic Thornton Brewery Building Getting New Life as Distillery," *Daily Southtown/Chicago Tribune*, February 23, 2017.

Bonansinga, Jay. 2004. *The Sinking of the Eastland, America's Forgotten Tragedy*. New York, NY: Citadel Press.

Romore, Kori and Brian Casella. "The Great Chicago Fire destroyed 17,450 buildings. Here are six that survived and still stand today." *Chicago Tribune*, September 28, 2021.

Pacyga, Dominic. **2015.** *Slaughterhouse: Chicago's Union Stock Yard and the World It Made*. Chicago: University of Chicago Press.

Higgins, Will. "The truths of the circus train crash of 1918 are more horrifying than the myths." *Indianapolis Star*, June 20, 2018.

Long, Carolyn Morrow. 2001. *Spiritual Merchants*. Knoxville, TN: The University of Tennessee Press.

Breo, Dennis and William Martin. 2015. *The Crime of the Century: Richard Speck and the Murders That Shocked the Nation*. New York: Skyhorse Publishing.

Bielski, Ursula. 1997. *Chicago Haunts*. Chicago: Lake Claremont Press.

Electronic sources

https://janeaddamshullhouse.org/history

https://www.hullhousemuseum.org/

www.lyonandhealy.com/history

www.oldstpats.org

ABC7chicago.com. "Walt Disney Childhood Home Renovated to Original Look," December 6, 2018.

www.jeppsonsmalort.com

Block Club Chicago, September 21, 2022 "Bob Newhart's Bizarre Commute Home to Edgewater Took Him WAY Out of His Way."

www.cbsnews.com. Local News. "Chicago Hauntings: The Horrors of the Iroquois Theater and Stories of Ghosts Left Behind." October 31, 2021.

www.screenwritersutopia.com. Donald Lorincz, student film for the Art Institute of Chicago.

www.route66news.com. "The Launching Pad Drive-In in Wilmington Il Closes," April 2023.

www.cbsnews.com. Local News. "Chicago Hauntings. L&L Tavern Known as the 'Creepiest Bar in the USA' for Reputed Visits by Serial Killers." October 22, 2021.

Personal Interviews for Book:

Ryan Graveface, Graveface Records, October 2022

John Holden, Edgewater Historical Society, 9/17/2022

John Hannafin, December 2017

Edward Maldonado, Clarke House, 2017

John Veliotis, Johnny O's Hot Dogs, 2016

Michael Figliulo, The Essanay Studios, 1989

Maurie Berman, Superdawg owner, 2014

Richard Brown, Newberry Library, January 2014

James Whiting, aka Sugar Blue, personal conversation

Dean Walter, Peacock Jewelers, March 2012

Index